Praise for Beverly D. Flaxington and "Understanding Ot'

"*Humans are strange creatures that are difficult*
'Understanding Other People: The Five Secrets
people who want to better understand these pec
ter every day. Drawing upon decades of experience, Beverly Flaxington encourages
readers to take her advice and apply it where they can. From better empathy to
avoiding mistakes, 'Understanding Other People' is a truly valuable read."

— Midwest Book Review

"*Beverly…defines successful relationships and how to nurture them…. Her book is a*
quick and easy read that will really make you think…and improve your life."

— Jordan Rich, WBZ Boston

"*In order to ascend the success ladder in business, personal*
ily harmony it's important to be able to communicate effec
what other people are trying to communicate to you.

DATE DUE

"*Finally, a new, effective communication model can b*
'Understanding Other People: The Five Secrets to Human B

"*The work provides information for empowering anyone*
Readers will learn how to understand the REAL meaning
saying. Information is provided about how to communic
your own REAL meaning, using powerful, motivating wor

"*This vital model is a fresh, understandable, effective wa*
common roadblocks to success."

— B. Nelson, Book Reviewer

"*This book really makes one stop and think about one's personal style and the im-*
pact it has on relationships. Beverly Flaxington does an excellent job of explaining
how the lens we use to see the world impacts the interactions we have with others.
Perhaps most importantly, she gives us valuable insight on how to adjust that lens
so we can be more positive and productive.

"*The book is an easy read, but it is packed with substance and real life examples that*
will be very familiar to almost anyone. What won't be familiar is the perspective the
author uses to analyze the things that make human interactions go off the tracks."

— Scott C. Sacco, Marketing and Communications Expert

Understanding Other People:

The Five Secrets to Human Behavior

How to stop being frustrated by the actions of others and
start taking charge of your own life — and reactions.

Beverly D. Flaxington

ATA Press

Published by ATA Press

ISBN 978-0-615-27229-0

First printing: April, 2009
Second edition: February, 2010

Table of Contents

This book is dedicated to the three people in my life who make every day a blessing—my children, Samantha, Kiernan, and Cynthia.

Foreword

I had the pleasure to evaluate Beverly Flaxington's book, *Understanding Other People: The Five Secrets of Human Behavior*, in a professional capacity. As I was reading it, to see if it would be of interest to our customers, I couldn't help but find myself deeply drawn to the concepts of the book and finding immediate application in my personal life.

Once you realize, for example, that most of us experience life through "all about me" filters, we gain a certain freedom in relationships. A freedom to stop feeling frustrated with another's actions and freedom to stop trying to have someone see your point of view. With this behind you, it really is easy to make progress in relationships, to reach true win-win solutions that take into account the other person's needs and motivations, and to operate from a positive sense of empathy and solution building. The concepts Bev describes in her book have been useful in all areas of my life with family members, clients, and business colleagues. I highly recommend this interesting, entertaining, and useful read!

Kim Guimond Dellarocca
Vice President, Marketing and Communications
Pershing LLC, a subsidiary of BNY Mellon

Introduction

People have asked me for years, "How can you get along with so many people?" "How can you negotiate and get what you want all the time?" "What's your secret?" The answer is not too complicated, and you're about to learn it! Once you understand what's happening in communication and in your relationships with others, you have a choice about what to do and how to gain a communication advantage!

I'm a career and behavioral coach, a corporate business consultant, a certified hypnotist and certified hypnosis trainer, a behavioral expert, a corporate trainer, a mom, and a college professor, and I've had years of corporate managerial experience — all of which together give me a unique perspective. When I was asked to teach a graduate course called "Dealing With Difficult People," I knew I had found my place. That's why I'm going to share my secrets with you — I hope you'll be able to internalize them and begin to use them in your day-to-day dealings.

For so many years I've watched people in work situations struggling to communicate, or I've watched people want to behave effectively in personal situations with a partner or within a team. Often I can see "both sides of the story" but can't figure out why one doesn't see the other's perspective! Over the years I've given so much feedback and offered so many insights into why someone else was behaving in a certain way that it seemed prudent to write down what I've observed in the hopes of sparing people pain in relationships — or at least give people some coping ideas when they find themselves in a difficult relationship.

The irony is that so many of our day-to-day interactions turn out to be "difficult." Even the people we *like* irk us sometimes! When you say "family" or "wife or husband" or "my teenage kid" or "my boss" or "my in-laws" to someone else, they'll often roll their eyes. Just identifying the relationships by their names brings a sense of unease or frustration. We struggle on a regular basis to make sense of other people and their viewpoints. Poor communication is at the root of so many of our pains and problems, and our lack of knowledge about what to do can paralyze us.

The most powerful people are the ones who understand themselves better than others understand them. This is because if we recognize what we are doing in our communications, and we can understand what others are doing, it gives us expanded choices in how to respond — and how to behave. The secret lies in how to achieve this power.

In this book I've taken decades of knowledge, observation, and personal and professional experience and rolled it all into five essential secrets. The beauty of learning them is that understanding and incorporating even one of the secrets will offer you the knowledge to make dramatic changes in your life and your relationships.

The best way to use this book is to digest one of the secrets at a time. Experiment with the secret: observe people and understand what the secret reveals about them. Then move on to the next one. Practicing and using these secrets will yield you information and give you enough insight to handle people differently in your next interaction.

I'm hoping the secrets you'll learn in this book will give you the tools and the information you need to understand those people you need to communicate with on a regular basis — and, just as importantly, to understand yourself more fully.

Secret Number One:
It's All About ME!

Secret Number Two:
Our Behavioral Styles Come Between Us

Secret Number Three:
Your Values Speak Louder Than You Do

Secret Number Four:
Don't Assume I Know What You Mean

Secret Number Five:
I'm Okay, You Are Most Definitely NOT Okay

Putting It All Together:
What To Do Next

Secret Number One:
It's All About Me

A h, the first secret — we could really just stop here and allow all of the secrets of the universe to be imbedded in this chapter, because each of us walks around all day long unconsciously repeating the mantra, "It's All About Me." Now we don't actually say this to ourselves, of course, but it's the message that underwrites everything that we do.

This is a hard concept for most of us to accept because it says that I'm focused — almost all of the time — on just me. We don't like to believe this about ourselves — after all, it sounds so ego-centric, doesn't it? But the truth is that when we're really honest with ourselves, we see that every thought we have, every experience we go into, we color with "*me*."

What does "It's All About Me" really mean? Are we really so self-obsessed? Well, yes, we are. Basically it comes down to the fact that we all — unintentionally — view every experience through our own lenses. It's not that we try to do this, or that we're bad people; it's just that we have no choice, because we are unaware of what we're doing and how we are behaving. We have all developed a set of experiences, a viewpoint of our understanding, and a perspective on the world that naturally colors every "new" situation we go into. Everything we see, say, hear, and do gets filtered through the mechanism I call "*me!*"

The Clogged Filters

The filters we've developed stand between us and everyone we meet. Why do I call them "filters," you ask? After all, I'm not a humidifier or drying machine! Too bad, because it would actually be nice to be able to remove those filters and clean them. If we could, each new experience would actually be "new" and not a redo of something we've seen or experienced in the past. It can't work this way, though — the problem for us humans is that our filters are invisible. If we could remove our filters and hold them up to the light, we'd be able to see the things that have clogged them up and realize that we simply can't, and don't, see clearly without "*me*" in the middle of everything.

What this means on a day-to-day basis is that, as hard as I may try to look at something with an objective eye, I can't. I see whatever I see through the lens called "me". Unintentionally, I color all of the events I encounter with my own expectations, my own beliefs, and my own concerns and needs.

All rolled into the filter is the combination of our past experiences, our view of the world, our concepts of right and wrong, our behavioral preferences, and our values (which we'll talk about in later Secrets in more detail). And, depending on your viewpoint, they could be clogged with astrological or numerical inferences, but one thing is certain — they are clogged!

If we imagine the filter to be a tangible thing that we can touch, we see that our filters are "in front" of everyone at every point in time. It's actually impossible for us to see anything clearly — a person, an event — because our filters stand in the way. The problem we have in communicating is that each of us has our own filter, and none of those filters can be clear and objective.

Think about it — two clogged filters trying to "connect" and gain an understanding of one another. It's a wonder we ever have any real communication at all! We'd like to believe that we are seeing correctly, from the other person's perspective — and that our minds are "open" and accepting, but the truth is that we have our filters out in front of every interaction. When you say or do something, I can only hear and see it through my own vantage point, with my filter in front of my experience.

Most of the self-help books will tell you that all you need to do, in order to open communication and relate to others, is to "Step into the other person's shoes. Empathize with them." Okay, this sounds great but how do I do this when my filters belong to me — and only to me?! It's not that I don't want to step into your shoes; it's that I truly, honestly can't do it. Your shoes simply don't fit me, and I don't understand anything about those shoes.

Don't Say, "I Know What You Mean"

Oftentimes the other person will get agitated if I say to them, "I know what you are feeling," or "I know what you mean." We don't like it when someone says this to us. Why? Aren't we happy that someone is trying to empathize with our position and "understand" us? No, we're not. When I say this to the other person, they believe that the focus is now on me — on the fact that I'm an understanding and empathetic person. I'm no longer focused on them, but rather have turned inward to check out my own feelings about what this person is saying to me. And, in reality, this is true! The other person feels this — they know I am no longer focused on hearing what they are sharing, but rather am having my own experience about what they are saying. Because, for both sides of the relationship and communication, it's all about *me*! So it's actually the kinder thing not to tell someone you "understand" because all you can possibly understand is your own experience — not theirs. And telling anyone that you have had a similar situation and can relate to what they are experiencing — and then proceeding to share everything about your similar experience — really isn't kind at all. If I start to do this, without meaning to, it turns the conversation right back from listening to you, to a focus on me.

Judging Others in Relation to "Me"

When I look out at you and have an opinion or a judgment about who you are, or what you're doing — I'm making that judgment about you in relation to *me*! We really don't have an opinion about others — we have the opinion relative to what they look like through our filter. This may be a hard concept to grasp (and admit) but it's really the truth. Why do

I say this? Think about how often you have the same experience of certain people — it's common knowledge that "like attracts like." Or that "we get what we expect." These aren't just pat little ditties that people say; they've come about because of their truth!

Do you know, or know of, anyone who has been married two or three times — to different people — but in reality it seems they have been married to the same person when we hear them talk about their current spouse? Why? Because the experience — the view they have of the other person — is colored by their filters and how they interpret the other person relative to themselves. They may even choose a similar spouse again and again, because those cloudy filters make it difficult to "see" that the person is essentially the same. Without learning how to recognize and become aware of the filters, in order to see more clearly, they will keep making the same muddled choices over and over. The same concept could apply to someone who has had several jobs and they've never been able to get along with the boss — "They're all stupid!" Isn't it possible that all the bosses aren't really stupid, but the filter the person is looking through is filled with "Stupid Boss" all over it? Yes, the bosses definitely all look stupid then!

Why Can't I See You Clearly?

The interesting thing is that we don't notice that our own filters aren't the same as the other person we communicate with — in fact, we instinctively believe that everyone does (or should) view the world the same way that we do! Why wouldn't everyone, when we know that we're right? We approach other people with our viewpoint of how they should react. When we don't get what we expect (and think about how rarely you *do* get what you expect), we get angry, frustrated, and disgusted with the other person.

Sometimes we turn inward on ourselves — frustrated that we didn't behave in a way we had expected we would. We criticize our own behavior in the relationship. We don't realize that our complaining stems from the fact that we didn't get a response or a reply that fits into our schema of how it should be. When this happens, we're even more convinced that the other person has a problem — or that we do. We don't see that if we didn't have our opinion of what we should expect, or what others are doing, there actually wouldn't even be a problem. The problem lies in my viewpoint — my clouded, clogged filter. It's the way I see things — or, in most cases, don't see things — that is creating my experience.

Filters Prevent New Information

The truth is that everyone *does* have their own individual filter that belongs to that person and is different from anyone else. In reality, we have no "new" experiences because everything we experience, each step we take, and each so-called new situation we enter has a filter in front of it.

We are almost never, without being very conscious, able to experience anything as "new." We go into every situation with our filter clogging what we are about to "see." So, it's my filter that's actually telling me what I am "seeing" — and what I'm seeing is a reflection back on me, of what I believe, expect, and know to be true.

Even my own sister has a filter filled with different experiences, behavioral styles, and values than my own. We may have grown up in the same environment with the same set of parents, but how we experienced those early years, everything that happened to us, and any other events or influences, makes us very different people with very different filters on the world. If my father said to both of us, "You're stupid!" my sister might have reacted by thinking to herself, "I'm stupid. I guess I can't do anything right." While I might have reacted by saying directly to my father, "You are a poor judge of people! You don't know what you are talking about!" Then I would take my next steps to show him how smart I am.

Those two very different filters — on the same comment, from the same father — would mean a world of difference in terms of how we then go about "proving" our experience. She may then suffer in situations, feeling unconfident, while I set out to prove how smart I am and to prove my father wrong.

Neither approach is "right" or "wrong" — it just is! But the results will be vastly different as we are going about the world with our individual filters in front of us. And where did the original filters come from? Well, anyone who has children knows that each child carries a different filter from that of their siblings, so we build those filters in very early on in life. Even in a family, no matter how similar the lifestyle may look from the outside, the filter each person has is filled with different things.

Look and "See"?

What are these filters all about? And how do they impact us on a day-to-day basis in our relationships? Let's walk through an interaction to understand how they work. I look out and see something (a combination of what's really there, and what I've made up — we'll talk about that in a moment). I make assumptions about what I see (using my ever-present filter to screen out anything that doesn't apply to me or doesn't fit my preconceived ideas), I apply my broad-based assumptions to whatever it is, and then draw my conclusion. And I *know* what I see — so don't try and tell me it's different!

For example, I may be a person who believes that all television reporters are very smart and knowledgeable about world events. I meet one at a dinner party and immediately put my filter up about what I expect. I might be with a friend who *is* truly knowledgeable about something that's happening in the world that we're all discussing, and my friend quickly realizes that the television personality doesn't know what they are talking about.

Well, my filter sits firmly in place and so I'd rather believe my friend to be misguided and to have made a mistake in this situation, than to have to give up my belief about TV reporters. As much as my friend could try and convince me — show me "facts" to the contrary, etc. — it will be very hard to move me away from my preconceived idea about how things should be.

This is what's so funny about "facts and data." Someone might say, "The facts don't lie." But do they? If I choose to disregard those facts, or I don't believe those facts are true for me, then are they really so set in stone? My friend has all of the data and details on why this television person has to be wrong and while I may listen politely, my filter is telling me, "She is my friend, but she is misguided in this situation."

This is really the curious thing about human beings: We are so adamant that we see clearly! We don't want anyone telling us that what we see isn't really real. It isn't — it's a picture of something shaded, colored, and skewed by the invisible filter we have sitting in front of our face (that's invisible even to me as I look through it!). I may eventually believe something else to be true, but if we go back to the television reporter example, I will find a way to explain that event. "That person just didn't understand." Or, "My friend didn't talk about it all clearly enough." We will still find a way to make sense of our preexisting ideas and convictions so that our ever-present filters will stay in place.

It's a fact that we need our filters to stay in place — it's a way to make sense of the world, and who we are in it. When we recognize this dynamic, we can begin to make changes; but until we do, the filters tell us how to behave and who we should be.

Who is Talking to You?

In hypnosis we have a concept called "self-talk" — it's the words rolling around inside of my own head all of the time, talking to me about this, that, and the other thing. Some people will refer to this as the "tapes" that we play, our very own personal MP3 downloaded perpetually into our brains. Sometime it feels like a group of your advisors — perhaps it's your mom, working with your church leader, your friends from the past, a boss who didn't like you, and maybe an ex-lover or an old friend thrown in for good measure! This group gets together and tells you what you should think, feel, and experience about everything. The voices get so loud sometimes that it's almost impossible to hear what you really think. And they talk all of the time.

The group in your head rarely takes a break from telling you what you are experiencing every step of your day. If you begin to listen to this group talking, you'll notice they have an opinion and an experience about everything. The one thing you can count on from the group is that they will always be talking about things that somehow revolve around you, and the impact on you. The group ensures our entire life stays focused on what's "all about me."

There are lots of positive thinkers out there who will teach you how to replace the talk with "positive self-talk." The theory goes something like this: Instead of saying "I'm unconfident. My father always told me how stupid I am," you replace this chatter with, "I'm a confident person. I know what I need to do and I do it. My father was a good man, but misguided in his thinking." While this does work to make you feel better, and probably to accomplish what you need to get done, the problem is that you are still talking *to* yourself, *about* yourself. The chatter is constantly telling us who we are, what we are seeing, and what's happening out there in the world. While it may be a good idea to talk about yourself more positively, it's a better idea to learn how to stop talking about yourself at all and just start experiencing life! We'll talk about how to deal with Secret Number One later, but one of the keys to really changing is to stop talking at all. Work on going quiet — both inside your head and even outside sometimes.

"Going quiet" can be easy to say, harder to do.

Same Teacher, Different Experiences

Let's apply how we all see the world through our own filters as it might unfold in my teaching experience: When I teach a class and the new students come in to learn, one person finds the information I am sharing new and exciting and they can't wait to employ it. Another person finds it boring and unnecessary, and a third person doesn't like the sound of my voice so he hasn't listened to a word I've said. How can three people in a room listen to the same speaker and come away with three radically different impressions of what they've heard? Aren't I the same teacher saying the exact same things to all of the students sitting there listening?

Of course, but the filters each person has put up in front of their experiences before I even open my mouth to begin to speak only allow them to see me in one way. The way I may look to someone is interpreted a certain way by that person, the way I start the class will mean something different to another, and the look on my face will mean something else to a third. *How*? Because, depending on their individual filters, they've had an experience with "someone like this" before and they know what to expect.

Define "Difficult"

At the start of our class on "Dealing With Difficult People," we try to come up with one clear way to define "the difficult" and we quickly find it's hard to do. As we put up traits on the white board, one person finds someone who doesn't listen difficult to get along with, but another person doesn't care about that and doesn't consider that "difficult." Another person finds people who are "pushy" difficult, but someone else finds them bold and definitive! The definitions of "difficult" are as varied as the students in the room.

Think about your own life — have you ever heard about someone who is described as "difficult" from a friend or a colleague, and then you meet them and find they are someone you enjoy being with very much? You simply can't understand why someone else would have described this delightful (in your filter) person as "difficult" — and, in fact, you'll go back and try and change the mind of the person who steered you wrong! You hope to go back and fix their misguided filter on it.

Haven't we all had the experience of someone telling us about another person, whom we know, that they really dislike? We can't believe they are talking about the person that *we* know, because we like them so much. It's all a result of our filters. What I think is "good," you may label as "bad." What I experience as positive action, you may interpret as negative — depending on what we have clogging our filters and the beliefs about life and people that are stuffed in there.

Stop Being so Rude! Oh…Never Mind

My favorite experience of this, and one I have had a number of times, is when I am driving in my car. I have a filter around "rude" people and I watch for them as I drive. I practice going quiet in my car a lot, and it's the place I personally struggle the most with applying my knowledge to start removing the filters in front of my experiences.

Once in a while, in my neighborhood, a car will come fast out of a street. I've almost been hit a number of times. My "rude" filter will immediately display and I will start to feel myself getting angry, until I realize it is my neighbor whom I adore behind the wheel of the car. All of a sudden, my filter moves to, "She must be having a hard day with the kids and be in a hurry. That's not like her to drive so quickly." I then wave her along with a big smile and go on my way.

Huh? This doesn't even make any sense. How did the "rude" driver turn into my neighbor and friend and someone I can smile at, even though she almost hit my car? My filters. The viewpoint I have about people I like, and people I know. They aren't the same "rude" people as all the others out there driving around that I don't know.

And, of course this applies in the opposite, too — when we know someone too well. My husband could say something in jest and mean well by it, and I may get frustrated with him because I think I know him so well and what he "really means," but a client of mine could say the exact same thing, and I listen intently and believe them to be smart! It's all about the processing mechanism, the filter we pass the experience through that determines how we will experience the outcome.

What is My Experience?

If you begin to pay attention to this, you'll find these experiences all day long, every day. A crying baby in a restaurant is "annoying" to one patron who doesn't like children, or who hasn't had enough sleep and has a headache. The same child is "beautiful" to another patron, perhaps a woman who always wanted children and couldn't have them. It goes on and on — the experiences are the same.

They are what they are, in this case: Restaurant. Crying child. End of the story. But it isn't the end — it's only the beginning in terms of what we do with the story, how we take it through our filter and make it into something.

Let's even extend the crying baby scenario. It's a husband and wife at dinner. She is sad because she can't have children and she loves to listen to the baby cry just to be near a child. He has a headache and is tired of hearing about babies and wants to just leave the restaurant. They aren't even speaking by the time they leave, and why? Because a baby cried and they extended the experience through each of their own filters and then onto one another.

We do this unconsciously each moment of our day. We're so wrapped up in "it's all about me" that we don't realize how much of every experience is just *us*. We can't possibly view and understand things exactly as someone else is doing — even when the people we care about try to make us understand as they do — because each filter is individual and different. By definition, the resulting experience will be different.

Just See it MY Way!

"What's the problem?" you may ask. "So what if I see things my way and everyone else sees things their way?" Well, ask yourself how much time we spend trying to sway each other's viewpoint. It's all about me, so I want you to see it the same way that I see it, and I won't rest until you admit that I'm right!

Think about this — we argue, we cajole, and we become incredulous because we're talking to someone who was in the same place we were in, listening to the same person we were listening to, and yet our experience of that person or event was so totally different. And I'm working hard to help you see the error of your ways.

Once you let the idea of this secret settle in and work with it, you'll start to see how silly it is to even waste the energy to make the other person "see" differently. They won't. They can't. And if you drop your need to make them see it, let go of your own need to be right about what you've seen and convince them of it — you'll conserve your own energy and attention for more important things.

Accepting Secret Number One and learning to understand that other people have their own filter that differs from the one you have, releases you from spending your whole life trying to convince others of what they've seen, what they should believe, and how they should behave. It releases you from needing the world to be the way that you want it to be and everyone in it to act like you. No one else — really no one — can see and understand everything just as you know it to be. Just having the knowledge that the other people out there are operating with their own filters can remove years and years of struggle trying to change someone else's mind about what they've experienced.

Who Defines the "Facts"?

Where we run into difficulty in our lives is when we are convinced that we see clearly and we know the facts of a situation, and it is our job, even our responsibility, to have others around us believe those same facts. Because, no matter what, the facts always exist, right? Something is red, or three feet long, or a solid substance, or beautiful, and that's what I see — but wait, "beautiful?" Is that a fact? Nope, the color, length, and composition are facts; the adjective "beautiful" is my label, but I believe it to be a fact and I will label it as a fact.

The "facts" may be there (red, three feet long, and a solid substance are factual statements), but after we give meaning to them, they become our facts. We can take something that is factual and provable, and make it into something specific to our likes or dislikes — so again, we can argue and disagree with someone else who sees it differently. For example, if we like something that's red, then the fact (through our filter) is that "red is a pretty color." If three feet seems like a lot to us, then "three feet is big." These become facts with our qualitative descriptors attached. We lose the ability to distinguish between fact and our perception. And, of course, our meaning and our labels result from those nice little filters that work 24/7 on our behalf. But when we go through life unaware of the "it's all about me" filtering process, it actually alters our reality and that of others. Reality isn't anything "real" anymore — it's just my clogged filter and my labels.

It *Is* All About Me!

The "all about me" philosophy applies to so many aspects of our lives that we're completely unaware of. If we stop and examine what we are doing and why we are doing it, and if we are really honest with ourselves, we quickly realize that we make all of our choices because of how it's going to impact *me*. Every consideration I give to something I am about to do, I color with "How will this affect me?" or "How will I look when I do this?" As an example, there are lots of people who are giving and caring and self-sacrificing, but even if we're those folks who focus on others and do nice things for other people, we'll realize we do everything because it's what we need to do for ourselves.

If I do a nice deed for you — maybe it's because I'm genuine sweetness and light (at least this is what I believe about me), but on the other hand maybe it's because I want to view myself as a "helpful" or "giving" person. I do the things I do not only because of the joy of helping or giving (although this can be an additional benefit) but because I like the feeling of being a "helping" person. My filter on myself is, "I'm nice and I help people because it's the right thing to do." I like to view myself through this lens, and I'll do whatever I need to do to ensure this self-image is intact. Even though I'm helping you, the truth is that it's still "all about me" — about me being a helpful person, about me being "nice," and about me being a giving and kind individual. I think about my own self-image the whole time I am helping you. Now, I'm not saying this is "bad" or "good" — it just is. Sure, we helper-types have helped someone in the process and done a good deed. But at the bottom of it, we're doing it to keep an image we have of ourselves intact.

You Better Appreciate What I've Done For You

If you want to prove this is true, think about some time you've done something for someone and they didn't appreciate it — or at least didn't acknowledge to you that they appreciated it. Most of us will get a bit miffed that we put ourselves out and didn't get the recognition. "Heck, I did that nice thing and they didn't even have the courtesy to say 'thank you'." So who is the "good deed" all about? If it's just about you and doing something for you, then why do I really care if I was rewarded somehow?

While it's hard to accept, we have to let ourselves see that we do it for me, not really for anyone else at all. There will be someone reading this who says, "That's why I give a lot of money to good causes anonymously — because it isn't about me getting the credit." And that's okay — but you still receive an intrinsic benefit and feeling of "I am a nice and giving person." Again, this is fine — a "good deed" was done (in my frame — some people would say that it is "stupid" to give away your money)! My goal here is just to point out that we are behaving in a somewhat mechanical fashion, letting our filters tell us what life is all about.

We've spent time and energy to create the self-image we have now and we don't want anyone to rock our boat — after all, if I'm not who I think I am, then who am I? Is it bad if I have this image of myself as being one way or another? Am I telling you that you shouldn't do nice things? Or that you shouldn't have preconceived ideas about whether red is a "nice" color or not? No, not at all. I'm not labeling anything here — as far as I'm concerned it's not bad nor good, it just is! It's simply that we are so unconscious of the mental processing going on all day long within the frame of what we refer to as "our experience" that perhaps we should become more conscious so we have more choices about how to act, and react, in our day-to-day lives.

But You'd Better Agree with ME!

The real problem comes when you express an image of me that doesn't agree with the self-image I have. I will rail against anyone who doesn't agree with my self-image as viewed through my filter (think of your last difficult exchange with your spouse, or your child, or your boss!). That's because "it's all about me" — instead of listening to you and trying to understand why you're saying what you're saying (who cares about *your* experience anyway?), I'm working hard to keep my "*me*" in place. Why do the people closest to us have such an ability to push our buttons? Because they know all about us! They have had the opportunity to see firsthand how we view ourselves and the world around us. Whether meaning to or not, those people who are close to us can find a way to bring something to light that we would prefer to keep hidden. Instead of seeing what's being brought up inside of us, we just see me getting disturbed. It's why we move into the vicious cycle of bad communication time and time again with the same people.

As I am writing this book, I've had a firsthand experience of this exact situation. When I put up a Facebook page, I had someone who sat next to me in English Literature in college thirty years ago seek me out. His view of me (from thirty years ago) is that I am "serious and focused." It's come through a number of times as we catch up on what we are doing. Now, I find this laughable because I've always been the person everyone comments on about my laughter and I rarely have a serious moment. I had a boss who told me I "laughed too much to be working hard" (his filter). But, hard as I try, I cannot get this Facebook friend to see me as a humorous person — I am "serious" in his mind. Every reply I give only seems to cement this image. It's a perfect example of the filters. Am I "serious"? Am I a "joker" instead? Well, neither one — and both!

Everything depends on the situation and the viewpoint. It's interesting, because maybe the person writing on my Facebook page thinks "serious" is a compliment! But to me, it's not a positive thing and I don't associate it with my own self-image. Yet to him, I am serious. But because "it's all about me," it bothers me that there is a misconception and I will take steps to convince him that I'm not a "serious" person. Hopefully you see the futility in this — I might expend all of this energy to talk someone else out of an experience they are having — and will I be successful? Of course not! His filter is one viewpoint and for him, it is true. My filter is another and for me, it is true. Neither of us is wrong — and even if we try to convince the other they are wrong, neither can get the real picture through the other person's filter.

You Make Me Feel Like..

Anyone who has gone through communication training has been taught to use "I messages." "I messages" go like this: "When you do that, it makes me feel like this." Have you ever tried using this in a heated exchange? It doesn't work, does it? You know why? Sure you do, because you now have one of the Five Secrets — it's because even when you use "I messages," it's still *all about me!* In fact it's even more about "me."

If I'm unaware of the filters, when I try to focus on you and listen to you, I really can't hear you. Now I'm focused on my "I messages" and making sure I am communicating clearly and in the right manner. I may even put on a layer of judgment that I am the one approaching our heated exchange in a clear and thoughtful manner and you are the bad guy.

Unless we take our *me* out of the picture entirely, we really can't get clear communication through our filters. Simply put: I hear what you are saying relative to what I believe, think, or feel. It's not that I don't care — really — it's that I can't put *me* aside long enough to just focus on you. Here I am hoping to incorporate my "I messages" to show you that I'm listening to you, but I need you to stop talking so I can use what I've learned. Oh, excuse me. Did you say something?

This is why active listening and reflective listening are so difficult for so many of us. Active listening really requires us to put aside our own beliefs or need to verbally jump in, and focus on what someone else is trying to communicate. It requires energy and attention that we aren't often willing to give to another person. Putting "me" aside and listening actively really *is* an active process. I have to stay continually aware of you, and of my filters creeping in to block what you are saying and preventing me from hearing your perspective, and your thoughts.

When we do reflective listening, it means I need to repeat back to you, in my own words, what I believe I heard you say. If you still question the truth of these filters, then observe what happens next time you try to explain something to someone else. It's a rare situation indeed when someone won't filter back their viewpoint, their experience of a similar thing! We will offer our own perspective on the other person's situation, but relative to what we've done, or experienced, or believe. The next time someone does this, try to refrain from judging them; just watch how often it happens in your day-to-day exchanges. The more you become aware of other people doing this to you, the more aware you will be when you do it to others.

Step Outside of Yourself

In most of our communication I can't really understand what you're saying to me, and you can't understand what I'm saying to you, unless you and I are in pretty solid agreement about what we believe and what we're expressing. This is why we love our long-time friends, or people we meet that are like us. If we're not in fundamental agreement, I can listen all day long but not really get to a level of understanding with you (unless I am working actively and taking my filters out of the way the entire time I focus on what you're saying).

What's the solution? Just stop talking with everyone? Well, we can't do that — after all, this is a book about understanding other people. And the truth is that it's in our interactions with others that we learn the most about ourselves. If we just sat with our own thoughts, feelings, and beliefs every day, we'd never learn anything!

What we have to learn is the art of somehow stepping outside of ourselves and really concentrating with singular focus on what the other person is saying. Only with lots of practice — on a committed and continued basis — can we accomplish this.

We know from behavior modification studies that in order to make any change more permanent, we have to practice with it consistently for a minimum of 21 days. To become a really dedicated listener would mean dropping my filters, and putting energy on others when they speak, for 21 consecutive days. That's hard to do because it does require tremendous energy to stay involved in another person, instead of wrapped up in our ever-present filters on the world. But the only way we stand a chance of being a more involved and communicative person is to go through the process of learning to focus, learning to listen, and learning to drop our filters.

At the end of the chapter, we'll talk about steps to take to incorporate this information. For now, though, the next time you have a discussion with a friend, or family member, or colleague, use your energy to stay attentive to what they are saying. Be aware of where your mind goes, or your "beliefs" about that person, and what they have to say. See if you can look at them with a new eye — maybe as someone you don't know anything about and want to learn more about. The more you do this, the easier it does become. Our lives can be so busy and so filled, we don't take the time to really connect and focus with others, and then we wonder why our relationships are suffering!

How Easy is it to "Sell" You?

This "all about me" psychological process also comes into play when someone is trying to "sell" you something. It's difficult to "sell" me if I can't understand why something makes sense for *me*. I want you to make the connection — help me understand why I should care. We'll talk more about making the connection for others in Secret Number Four, but for now let's focus on the part where it's all about me! So your vacuum cleaner has 12 nozzles and my existing vacuum only has 6? Why should I care? That's a feature, not a benefit to me!

Most companies never bother to figure out why I even care about what they're selling — many times they are just trying to appeal to some emotional connection for me. Show me the beautifully cleaned home, show me the happy family playing board games on the rug — and hope that I don't ask why I really should care about 12 nozzles. If I'm seeking a saner, happier life, the picture you've painted for me will resonate for me, but if by contrast I'm content with the cleanliness of my house — I'll hardly notice you were even talking!

So if the companies marketing to me help me see how their product will make me look and feel differently (and different in a "good way" as judged by *me*), I'm more likely to be drawn to purchase it. How will my life change? If it's in a way that I'm seeking, I'll buy the product. We're always seeking the next solution, the next product that will be that magic bullet for us to fix all of our ills.

If you can deliver a message or imagery to me that hits on some of those filters that are paining me, you have me hooked. Of course, if I'm an aware person realizing that you're doing this to me, I'll think twice about whether it's something I really need or want. So, even though the product or service often doesn't take me to nirvana, I don't care — I'll just keep looking for the next solution. (Who are all of those people in the ads where the wrinkle care cream made such a difference? Do you actually know any of them?)

Whose Side am I on Anyway?

In my consulting business, we observe the Five Secrets at work in many of our corporate situations with clients. It's not just in the personal relationship arena that these secrets apply. As an example, in many client situations we are asked to help with compensation programs. It's always interesting to me to see the position the employees often take: "I deserve this amount of money;" and the position management takes: "Don't they understand we're trying to make a profit here!?"

Both sides can see their own viewpoint (*me!*), but neither side will comprehend the perspective of the other. It's as if by admitting there is another view, it means that they have to accept that view. And yet for most of us, when someone else acknowledges that we have a point and a rationale for what we value, immediately we warm up to that person and are more willing to embrace their point of view.

In the compensation example just given, in my role as outside consultant, if I share the employee's viewpoint (and I may agree with some of what they say), management will respond that the employees have "convinced" me of something. If I share management's view (and I may agree with some of what they say) to the employees, they will think I am being paid by management to do what they ask me to.

It never occurs to either party that I understand both views and am trying to forge a conclusion that values both sides. Management may label the employees as "greedy" and the employees view management as "tightwads." With both sides labeling and taking a negative viewpoint, they aren't allowing communication and understanding to take place at all. The filter is so entrenched by both parties that reaching a win-win can take a lot of time and effort!

This happens in corporate life all of the time. We generalize our experience of "management," or of "labor unions." It never occurs to us that there are many exceptions to any rule, so we enter into our negotiations or our dialogue with a focus on "me" and a belief about "them" that hampers our ability to have a real exchange.

If we could put aside *me* and my filter for a moment, and "see" the other person as having a right to their position, perspective, or ideas, we would find ourselves in many more situations having the "Aha!" of understanding.

Watch Your Labels

Take a minute to think about the process that goes in inside our own heads. We look out at reality, we filter it, and then we label it. It's a three-step process that we're completely unaware of. Once we hit that third step and apply our label, we'll connect it to something else in our awareness. At this point we connect other things to it — sometimes called "triggers" (anything you can think of that "sets you off?").

Now we're so deep into our own world that we can't be objective, and our emotional thoughts take us over. As a hypnotist, I can also say it's a form of hypnosis: I don't really "see" what's out there but rather am walking around in what we call a "trance state."

I'm thrown this way and that by my experiences and my feelings because of the triggers that can set me off: "Why did he say that? What a jerk;" "This stuff can't work for me — it's too complicated;" "I find this interesting and wonder about exciting ways to use new information — let me experiment with this;" "Why in the world would anyone want to go out wearing that? What an idiot."

We self-talk and lull ourselves into a state where we really believe what we see is real, and we're right about it. I don't know about you, but I get tired of myself sometimes. I don't want a world where everything I see is all about me.

Begin to Pay Attention

So how do you use Secret Number One to your benefit in your day-to-day life? Pay attention to what people are saying and doing, and practice doing so without putting a label on anything or trying to sum up, in your own experience, what you see. Admit that "it's all about me" for you — and use your energy to put *me* aside and focus on someone else. Realize how your filters play into every exchange.

Think about the labels you put on things — is it "good" or "bad" or does it make you "happy" or "sad?" Why? What's happening to create the emotion in you, and why do you have a need to label everything? Do you always react the same way to your child? Your spouse? Your boss or the co-worker in the other cubicle? Why? What is it about them that sets you off? You'll notice that you want to explain it's about *them*, when in fact (and now you know), it's really all about *me*. I read a column in the local paper where people write in to ask how to deal with their "difficult co-workers," and I always want to find that co-worker that's being reported and ask if they have difficulty with the person writing in!? Whenever we hear both sides of a story, we realize there is merit to each side. Why are there two sides in the first place — that's right, the two sets of filters!

To experiment with this secret, start to pay extra attention to anyone trying to sell you on some idea or something they care about. I like to practice when my 12-year-old daughter starts her "pitch" (my filter) on something she wants to do. If she hits certain buttons that resonate with me, mostly because the request is reasonable in my opinion, I'll readily agree. If I feel I am being snowballed (my filter), I'll dig my heels in with her, even though her request may be legitimate. I have to work very hard and put my attention completely on her and her request in order to avoid falling into either trap.

You'll begin to notice that if something presented to you connects with who you already think you are, or who you want to be — you'll likely go for it. If it doesn't, you won't even notice anyone is talking to you. Understanding the filter is powerful. Once you understand what's going on, you'll take back your power. Right now, every day (almost every minute of every day), you're giving it over to others. As long as we don't realize "It's All About Me," we'll keep responding in a mechanical fashion.

Watch What Others Do

If you want to learn how to avoid this, watch what other people do. Watch their reactions to things you say. Watch their reactions to other people. Are there people whom you can just predict how they are going to respond to a given stimuli? Observe "helpful" people or "giving" people, or "I feel sorry for myself" people. Watch what's going on with others and then step outside of yourself to see what's going on with you! In families or close relationships, it can be easy to observe this happening.

Is there anyone you know where a certain event, or trigger, or word will just "set them off"? It could be politics, religion, money, the economy, and so on, but certain people allow themselves to be baited into disagreeable discussions so easily and so predictably. Watch this when it happens with those people you know; watch the transformation take place and how that other person doesn't even know they are being swept away. Then watch yourself. Do you have any triggers like this? Become aware of what passes through the filter and how you judge it, before you react to it next time.

Find Your Triggers

And even though our filters stay in place, we all change roles, too. Sometimes I am the "martyr" and other times I may be the "victim." We aren't necessarily stuck in one role or one view of the world — we will change it around based upon the circumstances. What's fascinating is how unconsciously we do this, though. The incident goes like this: I feel sorry for myself; I'm overworked, underpaid, and generally taken advantage of in my life. I act this out with my spouse and he says, "Stop being a martyr. You're no different from anyone else." "What?! Me, a martyr? Never!" This doesn't reconcile with the filtered view I have of who I am. I'm not a martyr; I am a... [whatever my momentary self-view is]. It's my husband who is (obviously) the problem. He is putting labels on me that don't fit my own self-view.

Now, it's true that the other person *is* also labeling through their own filter. Maybe my husband's mother was a martyr type. Maybe it makes him feel so uncomfortable that he has to label me as "wrong." There could be lots of dynamics going on with him, but one thing is for sure: "It's all about me" on my side of the exchange, and "It's all about him" on his side of the exchange!

Whatever I've decided is *me* is what I center my universe around. We'd like to think it's our family, our children, and our friends — or our community as a whole — but, by and large, it's really about us. And if pressed to be honest, our family, children, and friends would say they see this, too! Tough to take? Not really, if we consider that just by understanding this and being willing to accept it (because it is true for all of us — especially when we are unaware of what is happening) we can move out of the stasis we live in and live differently. When we understand we are filtering, we can't change overnight but we can start to become more conscious of our thoughts and reactions, and how much "me" we have in all of them.

Change is Hard

The only way we will be able to open our communication more effectively, and understand ourselves and others, is to start to observe this filtering process in action. When we see the many ways, throughout our day, that we have "me" in front of every thought, and every action — we become more self-aware. Being self-aware gives us the information, and allows us a chance to make choices about how to behave differently. We may continue to fall into the same behaviors, but the more we see ourselves doing this — and make a decision to try again — the more we stand a chance of changing our interactions for better outcomes.

What to Do?

Now that we've covered the first secret, here are step-by-step instructions on how to use Secret Number One to your advantage (because it *is* all about you, right?).

This section, at the end of each of the five secrets, gives steps to take and ideas to implement so that you can learn more about whether these secrets apply to you and those you want to communicate with more effectively. While they sound simple, they are not as easy to implement. If you want to be effective, you may be trying to change a lifetime of behavior! Consider which actions you want to commit to and practice with one before you move on to the next one. Knowledge is power!

1. Watch others — become an interested observer in human nature. Now that you know it's all about them, observe how the people you know react to different things, and how often that reaction seems predetermined and predictable. If you know someone who always reacts a certain way to certain people (politically biased people from either party in particular are fun!), you can predict what will happen next. Watch what sets them off — what the "trigger" is that gets them back into a certain role time and time again. Be a watchful observer of people so that you can see how this dynamic plays out with others.

2. Next, watch your own reactions. What are you saying to yourself as someone else is talking to you? What are you saying to yourself as you're reading these words? What are you feeling when someone tells you something you don't believe about yourself? What do *they* see when they talk to you? Become an interested observer of your own thoughts and feelings and reactions to things. How predictable are you?

3. Recognize your own "triggers" — those things that set you off, or create a certain predictable reaction in you. Notice them, and then begin to pay attention to the triggers when you encounter them and see if you can catch your rote response before you go into it next time. Catching yourself before you respond in an unconscious fashion gives you more choices about how you'd like to react and behave with others.

4. Then, make a conscious decision to stop — yes, *stop*! Stop being who you are all of the time. Let yourself be no one for a while. Try to get rid of your preconceived ideas about what you need, who you are, and what you want to be. Just be. Wow — deep, huh? But how does one accomplish enlightenment? How does one just "be"? Well, save all of that money you think you'll have to spend on self-help courses to find out — all you have to do is

keep "stopping" all day long. Periodically, have those momentary meditations where you just let all of your thoughts leave with nothing in their space. Practice being an interested observer. Stop going along with whatever you believe yourself to be. Ignore the voices telling you what you see, what you think, and what's out there. Practice just observing — become like a detective, no preconceived ideas, no prejudged conclusion; just be on a quest to find the "facts and only the facts." Realize when you are labeling something and ask yourself why you have to apply the label. Experiment with just letting the color red be red, and not considering whether you "like" red or not!

5. In each interaction, really see other people. When someone talks to you, don't think about what you're going to say next. Drop the act. Drop the image you have of who you need to be when you're with them. Focus on the person across from you or on the other end of the phone. Watch who they are being. Learn what they are all about. There is probably no one individually more effective way of strengthening our relationships with others than putting our emotional energy into focusing on what they are saying and doing. The person, in any exchange, who has learned their own style and can recognize that of the other person (or people) will always have the power to communicate more effectively in the exchange.

Secret Number Two:
Our Behavioral Styles Come Between Us

In my consulting business we use a wonderful behavioral tool called DISC (which stands for Dominance, Influencing, Steadiness and Compliance). Many people know about this tool — it's been around for 30 years and has been statistically validated over and over again in 30 different countries. Our consulting firm is a distributor of the tool and I have been certified in using it through a company called Target Training International. Working with this tool has really opened my eyes to the power its impact on our communication approaches. As I discuss DISC and its application here, you'll hear about research I have access to — as well as my own interpretation and experiences.

"Can You Talk to My Spouse?"

I wish I had a dollar for every time we reveal someone's behavioral style with one of our corporate clients, in a business setting, and they say, "Can you have my spouse take this?" The person at our client firm who is taking the profile is able to review the results and have their own "Aha!" about what they do and how they act, and they will often ask us if their spouse could complete a profile, too. Our client seems to want their spouse to be able to have their own "Aha!" as well (or, probably more likely, they want their spouse to understand why they are the way they are and be more forgiving about their idiosyncrasies!). Even if the spouse doesn't complete a profile, our client will start to open up and share differences in style and approach — and issues they encounter — with their spouse as a result of behavioral mismatch.

We'll find we are in a formal business setting with very — often extremely — successful people supposedly to do an organizational review, or provide sales training, and instead, all of a sudden, they start asking us how we can help them use this information with their spouses! Why would successful businesspeople open up to us and start telling us about the issues they have at home?

Simple — they had an eye-opening experience once they learned about their own style within a framework to understand it. They realize that the other person (in this case, the spouse) is not deliberately trying to drive them crazy, but that the behavioral styles come between them. When they have this newfound information, they have a need to share this "Aha!" moment with someone who might understand.

The tool is typically completed online by responding to approximately ten minutes of questions about how I would behave in certain situations. After completion of the questionnaire, I receive a 20+ page profile with my particular behavioral characteristics. The importance of the information is that learning my DISC profile allows me to more objectively understand why I may communicate in a particular way and why someone else's communication style might be difficult for me. It's not that I don't intuitively know myself; it's just that I haven't had an organized way to understand why I conflict with other individuals so often and in so many ways. Behavioral style is often at the root of our differences.

Of course, most people we work with just love taking the profile survey and getting their personal results. Do you know why? Easy! Because we all like to see information that revolves around us!

We All Fall Somewhere on the Behavioral Scales

There are different scales of behavior — different approaches we each take to solving problems, communicating, addressing an issue, or putting a plan together. The way we approach almost all of the life activities we do every day is usually a function of our natural behavioral style, or the way we are adapting in order to cope in a different environment. Behavioral style is one of those "secrets" that once you understand it, *so* much of what has been confusing about what other people do, or even why you do what you do, begins to make sense.

We behaviorally fall somewhere on each of the four scales, so in addition to how we might behave on any one scale, how they interact with one another also matters. To understand each scale let's go through a primer on behavioral style.

Introducing the DISC Model

There are four different modes of behavior tracked by DISC, and each behavior is rated low to high on a scale from 1-100. The point where 50 rests on the line is called the "energy line," or the mid-line, and behavioral style falls either above or below the line. The lower you go, the more extreme your behavior will be in one direction and the higher you go, the more extreme it is in the other direction. If someone is above the line, their behavior on that scale will be dramatically different from someone who falls below the line. This is where we experience our failures when trying to communicate — if we're on different sides of the line, or have otherwise different preferences of behavior, we communicate in very different ways.

As we'll discuss, there are people on one or more of the scales who are right in the middle — or at the line. These people will read the next section and may not feel that certain areas apply to them — they have more adaptability than those who are high in one direction, or low in another. Not knowing about style differences means we're doomed to miss the mark with some people — and understanding that these differences exist, offers us many more choices in our day-to-day interactions.

The Four P's of Behavior: Problems, People, Pace, and Procedures

To make it easy to recognize the four different scales (D, I, S, and C), we call them the "Four P's of Behavior." We look at Problems (the Dominance scale), People (the Interacting scale), Pace (the Steadiness scale), and Procedures (the Compliance, or Rules scale), and then assign rankings to people based on how they deal with these issues.

Where someone rates on each of the scales is key to their approach and their preferences. In fact, the DISC approach is an easy one to master because each of the scales has a tone of voice, preferred word choices, style of behavior (fast versus slow), and an emotion attached to it. Once we understand the different approaches, we can watch what someone does in their communication and understand their preference.

The D Scale — How you Handle Problems & Challenges

On the first scale, Dominance (D) — the scale looking at how we deal with Problems, when someone is a 60 or above on a scale of 0 — 100, you'll see a very assertive, very aggressive stance toward problems and challenges. These are folks who talk fast and move fast toward a task because they are very results-oriented, task-oriented, challenge-oriented, and physically aggressive. People high on this scale will tend to need physical activity to de-stress — for example, they may be marathon runners, or at the gym every day, or rock climbers, etc. They are motivated by challenges and once they've accomplished one thing — they are ready for the next.

Often a high D can come off as intimidating — they are focused on the task and want to *get something done!* If you or I stand in their way, they'll get irritated and upset at us for thwarting their plans. The high D wants to move quickly toward the task at hand — especially if it is a challenging task they are anxious to take on. Because of the craving for challenge, they see things as "bait" or challenges, even when someone doesn't intend them this way. They will be found on the debate team at school, because they often argue for the sake of arguing.

It's fun to see two high Ds who are really in agreement with one another — they'll disagree just because it's challenging! High Ds often appear impatient and even will seem to be looking for a fight. They don't shy away from conflict, and in fact they often embrace it because of the challenge involved. The high D sees something that needs to be done and because of their results-driven orientation, they move toward doing it. Things like data, thinking through the steps, considering what might go wrong and so on are often frustrating and unnecessary to a high D. At times, they tend to operate with the "shoot first and ask questions later" approach to life!

Each scale also has an emotion associated with it, and the D emotion is anger or frustration. You'll notice high D people getting easily upset when they are thwarted from getting to their results or their plans. If they are intent on finishing something and someone comes in and gets them off track, they'll show their frustration! And they are definitely the ones who get most visibly upset in traffic if the cars are moving slowly and they are late to get to some appointment!

If, however, you rate 40 or below (on all four scales, someone who is anywhere from 41 to 59 is right smack in the middle of the two styles and will have flexibility to go in either direction depending on the circumstances), then you are considered low D. This means that you are able to get to a result, but it's done in a much slower, more methodical, thoughtful, and data-oriented way. Their approach is not urgent, not angry, and is often put off by the very aggressive, hard-hitting style.

The lower D will tend to want to gather all of the info they need before they go off to implement a plan or a result. They want to be sure they have covered the bases and understand everything they need to understand. This means the style is much more slow-moving, slow-thinking, and slow to act. The low D operates with a very long fuse, choosing not to get upset or angry unless really, really pushed.

The High D, Low D Communication Confusion

The low D and high D have an obvious conflict. If I'm results-oriented, fast-talking, fast-moving, and focused on accomplishing the challenge before me and you are slower to act, more prone to think about things, and ask a number of questions for clarification *before* you act, we're going to drive one another crazy. The low D feels intimidated while the high D just wants to reach out and choke someone! It's next to impossible for each to see the other person's perspective.

The more the high D is getting angry and frustrated, the more the lower D is moving into their shell and wanting to avoid, avoid, and avoid some more. The high D will just shut down the low D in many situations. I've observed that it's easier (albeit frustrating) for the higher

D to pull back on the throttle than it is for the lower D to speed it up. Unfortunately for a high D, the more they pull the throttle back — especially for long periods of time — the more likely they are to just blow up when they can't take it anymore!

In work places this becomes so obvious when a meeting is held and one person (the higher D) has "heard enough" and just wants to rush out of the meeting to get moving on the project! The lower D person starts to ask even more questions, feeling a bit uneasy that the higher D is so anxious to move. So the higher D pulls back in and wants to push the lower D, while the lower D just can't understand why the higher D won't "calm down and just look at the data."

Once you understand this dynamic — between any of the two scales — you'll notice these behavioral mismatches going on all the time. And if you are one of those higher Ds whose spouse or kids say to them, "Stop yelling at me!" and you are thinking that you are *not* yelling — now you know why there might be a misunderstanding occurring!

The I Scale — How you Interact with and Influence Others

All of the preferences matter and interact with one another, so let's next look at the Influencing scale (I). This is a people orientation. High Is (again 60 and above) like people. In fact, they are energized by being around people. They gain energy by the experience of interacting with other people — kibitzing and talking about everything. Their focus is on "the experience." If I like what I'm doing and I'm enjoying myself, I don't care about much else going on. Because of this, high Is can lose track of time easily and become disorganized, since they are focused on having fun — having a good experience, while time escapes them.

The high I has good social capabilities — an ability to talk to people they don't know in an easy and comfortable manner. They also like people and they like people to like them. To be socially outcast is very painful for the high I, so they will go to great lengths to avoid upsetting someone, or having someone be mad with them. As such, in contrast to our high D, they will avoid conflict entirely. It's better just to avoid a difficult subject than to run the risk that the other person will be alienated.

Is are also very verbal — they need to talk about things — anything, anytime! It's hard for an I to process anything without the opportunity to discuss it in great detail. They can be verbally persuasive in their speaking, so they often find themselves in careers like sales, teaching, or public speaking, where they can use verbal skills to persuade someone to their way of thinking. The high I loves to talk — needs to talk, in fact. The higher the I, the greater the need.

The most obvious sign is when you know someone who seems to talk too much — or wants to talk about everything. And, generally you'll know a high I when you observe their emotional response: it involves an optimistic approach to life — the sky is blue and the grass on their side is already greener! They are positive and speak with positive terms. Often times you can locate them quickly in a company because they are in the cubicle from which laughter emanates and where lots of people gather around. The high I finds fun in everyday things and has a tendency toward laughter and enthusiasm.

One of the problems the higher I person can run into is that they often trust others too much — as a manager, it can be hard for them to use discipline because they always want to believe that someone is just about to turn around! They are always willing to give someone another chance and hope for the best (an optimistic viewpoint!). They expect others to trust them just because they say something is so — because of this, they will often trust others even when that trust may not be warranted.

By contrast, someone lower on the I scale, 40 or below, will tend to be much more reserved. They are more cautious in their approach to people. The lower I people are often tagged as "unfriendly," but often are not unfriendly so much as just not comfortable jawing it up with people they don't know well. And even when they do know someone well, they may not feel a burning desire to verbalize or participate in a discussion that's going on. They are more often than not the quiet ones in a meeting — observing, thinking, and paying attention to what's going on but not sharing their thoughts.

Some people may wonder why that low I isn't participating — it's not that they aren't involved, it's just that they don't have a compelling need to share a perspective. When they want to contribute they will, but they don't always need to.

The lower I is more skeptical and distrusting of others. They will tend to go into new social situations very slowly. They have little need to interact, and in fact can be drained by too much interaction with others. While the higher I is actually energized by interaction and needs people and stimulation, the lower I would rather have time alone. It's easy to see how there could be trouble at the dinner table if a high I and a lower I lived together!

A common couple dynamic is when a lower I has a job that requires them to interact, talk with others, and be generally in relationship all day. When that person comes home, they are drained and want some "quiet time." They may be married to a higher I. The higher I spouse is just waiting for the chance to "talk about our days." The lower I could think of nothing they want less than talk about their exhausting day. They just want to go internal and try and conserve their energy!! So the higher I feels they don't matter to their spouse, and the lower I feels drained by their spouse. Neither one feels like their needs are being met, or that they are "understood" by the other.

The lower I has a tendency to want data — again, their skepticism means that the more I try and convince them with my words, the less likely they actually are to believe what I am saying! Salespeople, beware! Usually you'll find salespeople on the higher I scale — it's a career that theoretically involves talking for a living. So, the high I salesperson has a natural tendency to want to talk more — to fill in the void when the other person doesn't respond.

The important thing to remember is that the more this happens with a lower I person, the less they actually believe you and feel connected. In fact, it's like two opposite magnets repelling one another. The more I, as a higher I salesperson, push and talk — the less you, as a lower I prospect, believe me and trust me.

The salesperson gets exactly the opposite of what they went into the meeting hoping to get. The lower I sees the salesperson as "pushy" and overly friendly and talkative — and of course the higher I sees the lower I prospect as unfriendly, unengaged, and unwilling to participate. It never occurs to either one that there is simply a behavioral mismatch. Instead we put the judgment, the "color," around the behavior and if it's different from our own — it must be "bad."

The Styles all Work Together

So let's look at the first two scales together. If I am high on the D scale, but also high on the I scale, I can drive to a result but with a smile on my face. However, if I'm high D and lower on the I scale, I am getting to the result and not being very friendly in the process. The first combination will be more "likeable" and the second less so. But can you see how the labels start to apply? It's my perception about the combination that I label.

In our society we value certain things and we tend to push away people who are "mean" and hard drivers in the process of getting there. But it is simply behavioral style in many cases that we're seeing and reacting to. It's the labels that push us further and further away from understanding this.

The High I versus Low I Communication Confusion

In a work setting the I disconnect may be an obvious one. Let's go back to the meeting scenario. Let's say we have a very high I in the room. This person will want to talk, ask questions, and share a personal experience about most things being discussed. If there are lower Is in the room, they will get annoyed or disturbed that the meeting isn't ending because someone needs to talk so much. Meanwhile the higher I is wondering why the lower I just doesn't seem to care and isn't participating. Both people think their approach is right and that the other person needs to shift behaviors.

The S Scale — How You Handle a Steady Pace

The next scale, "S," is about Steadiness and work environment. The high S individual has a number of facets connected to their style. They prefer predictability, stability, and having the boundaries of the pond defined. In other words, job descriptions, specific requirements, or expected deliverables — and knowing what is expected of them — are key with a high S. They will prefer sameness and predictability, but overall they don't resist change as much as they resist being changed.

The high S is very calm, nonemotional, and reserved. The emotion for this scale is actually nonemotional. Someone high on this scale will be very hard to read — you could give them wonderful, exciting news or give them the worst news ever, and they will show little difference in their emotional response. They can be perceived as "phlegmatic" and "calm" about everything going on in life. Because of this, they are often viewed as cold and uninvolved.

Again, it's not that this is true — it's just the nature of the style. While they may appear to be stand-offish, they are excellent listeners and can pay rapt attention for long periods of time. They are able to listen patiently and focus on what another person is saying without an emotional response, and without the need to jump in with their own thoughts. In an organization, they'll often be the "glue" person because everyone else seeks them out to tell their own personal tale of woe. We know, going into a high S's office, that they won't react strongly no matter what we say to them, and this can be a comfort to many people.

High S people move slowly, but with a people orientation. They are interested in the well-being of the team and the "family" — whether it be defined as work, or home-life family. We often counsel our clients to think carefully when firing a high S, because they'll find themselves losing the person who held everyone else's secrets. The high S knows all, but never tells anything. They are the keepers of information and, in most cases, hold everything they've ever received.

In one case we had a client with a very high S employee who quit and moved across the country. Afterwards, the client firm found every memo the firm had ever written and circulated in this person's office. He had kept absolutely everything — and, in some cases, was in possession of information that people in the firm had been looking for for months. While he was working there, they couldn't find the information, but it turned up the minute he had left and they cleaned out his office!

The high S likes closure, and with their process and organized approach will have several projects going at once and know exactly what step each project is in — and what needs to be done to reach the conclusion. They don't like to be interrupted, though, and they certainly don't want you to change things up while they are in the middle of their assigned projects. They prefer to have their list and be able to work at their own pace to complete each assigned task.

The downfall of the S is that they can accommodate others too much. They may even take on the work of others because they just can't say "No." They will do whatever is asked of them, and never complain about it. They are the people in an office who are working late hours finishing up a project that didn't even belong to them in the first place! They'll take on lots of work just to get things finished and closed-out. However, they may get to a point where they feel resentful because they've taken on too much!

By contrast, those people scoring low on the S scale are much more emotive and much more "heart on their sleeve" with their emotions. They will chafe at too much structure and look for situations with loose boundaries. Some lower S types will juggle many activities — and do it happily. They like to shake things up and change things, sometimes just for the sake of change.

A dynamic we frequently observe with our corporate clients is one in which the senior management staff is low on the S scale, moving quickly from activity to activity and changing their approach and priorities frequently, but their staff may be made up of higher S folks — the latter tend to choose admin roles and places where they are charged with process and getting things done.

The higher S has their projects all laid out in a neat, orderly fashion (color-coded files and everything, sometimes!) and then the low S "juggler" comes along and shakes it all up by assigning something new. It can be very stressful and distracting for the high S.

Many low S leaders will have a new idea and want everyone to switch gears and march in the new direction. But the high S folks need time — time to bring closure to what they've been doing, time to digest the new direction, and time to create a plan to implement the new ideas.

To get the best out of staff hired because of their process orientation, make sure to let them finish before asking them to move on to the next thing. Remember that the combination of nonemotional along with a need to accommodate means that the high S individual won't tell the boss this is what they need — just know that it is true!

The High S versus Low S Communication Confusion

To observe how this plays out in a meeting with the different styles, let's say there is a low S boss excitedly offering information about a change taking place in the organization. Here you'll find the higher S paying rapt attention to everything being said (they are excellent listeners). They won't show any emotional response to anything, however, so the lower S giving the presentation may perceive them as "disengaged" or "not interested." The two different people will leave the meeting wondering, "Why is he/she always like that?"

The low S is looking for an emotional reaction, and the high S will never give it to them — they can't! The lower S showed their enthusiasm for the project by wearing their heart on their sleeve throughout the discussion. The higher S listened intently and knows exactly what was said, but their body language and facial expressions did not give away whether they thought it was a great idea or not!

The C Scale — How you Handle Compliance, Rules, & Procedures

Last but not least, there is Compliance (C); following the rules and procedures set by others. The high C individual will tend to follow rules and procedures and be very loyal to authority without any questions, push-back, or back talk. C is also a quality-control scale and, as such, high Cs can come across as very critical — they have high standards for both themselves and others. One of their gifts is the ability to identify a problem right away. They can look at a set of issues or ideas and immediately pick out the one that won't work. They are often described as "nit-picky" but it's just their nature to find the missing thing — the thing that's wrong.

High Cs tend to work well alone. They are focused on quality and ensuring things are "right," and will work until all is done to standards. They often seek jobs where they are in charge of upholding the rules and procedures. Think about the military, compliance oversight, auditing, quality control or quality assurance, and airplane mechanics — all roles where focusing on doing it "by the book" is key. High Cs won't push back on authority and are very focused on doing what's right in the eyes of the people perceived to be in charge. The emotion for this scale is fear — fear of rule-breaking, or fear of authority. High C folks will offer immediate respect to anyone they perceive in an authoritative position. They actually have a fear that stems from the concern that authority will find them at fault for doing something wrong. Personally, because they care so much about things being done right and correctly, I would never want to get on an airplane that wasn't inspected by someone high on the C scale. These are people who take "making sure it is right" very seriously!

It can be very hard to "sell" a high C because they need a lot of data — sometimes they move into analysis paralysis — and sometimes it's simply because they like all the data. The more data they have, the more comfortable they feel. The high C will keep asking for data and information. Even when they've got a lot, they want to understand the next level of data! To force them to move — to make a decision — can be extremely time-consuming and difficult.

High C people, because of their need for quality and quality control, can be very hard on themselves. Their own performance is never up to their own internal standards. If you know someone who beats up on themselves a lot over mistakes they've made and can't seem to shake things off, they are likely high on this C scale.

The contrast to this — people who score low on the C scale — are creative problem-solvers. They chafe a bit at rules — at least those that don't make sense to them — and they will look for new and "better" ways to do things. Low C people tend to look for the new way, the different way, and (in their minds) the better way to do something. They don't want to flagrantly break rules (maybe sometimes they do!) but they do want to find a better way.

So in an organization, for example, a low C individual working for a high C person may be perceived as a "rebel." They aren't, in their minds; they are just very comfortable pushing back at authority, looking for new ways, and challenging the tried and true. And, in direct contrast to the fear of the high C, the low C is very comfortable telling the authority figures that they're wrong, or that there is a better way to do something. In a rules-based organization, they'll find themselves in trouble quite a bit. The low C folks don't care as much about data. They may gloss over too many fine points to find the data that they need!

High C versus Low C Communication Confusion

This disconnect in organizations — or between people — is most evidenced by the need to do things "right" versus the need to "find a new way." A higher C person believes that rules are there to be followed and that by breaking the rules, or disobeying the people in charge, you're doing something wrong, while a lower C person sees a rule as just a "guideline" or in some cases, just an "idea" to be discussed, considered, and potentially even disregarded!

Picture an auditor (higher C) coming into the office of a manager (lower C) who doesn't like to keep records, is doing some creative accounting to get close to the edge but not over it, and doesn't care much about the quality of the details. The two people are simply never going to see each other's viewpoint. The high C will believe the lower one to be in flagrant disregard of what matters. The lower C will think, "What a stick in the mud!"

I Want You to Act Like ME!

People — all kinds of people — function best if they can work within their own style and not adapt to someone else's. So as you learn this material and work with it, you may find it educational to watch the four different scales interacting with one another — such as a low and a high D, one getting frustrated (the high D) because things are not moving quickly enough, and the other feeling intimidated (the low D) and not understanding *why* the high D gets so upset all of the time.

And those Is — the high I with the need to verbalize about everything: talk, talk, and talk some more. They are very emotive, very fast-talking and fast-moving, and often talk with their hands and make lots of gestures when they are speaking. Contrast them in a meeting with a low I who only talks when they feel they have something important to say, and one of them can't understand why the other is so unfriendly, while the other thinks to himself, "Shut up!"

The S difference — one is slow-paced, methodical, and keeps their emotions to themselves, the other is fast-paced and can't wait to tell you all about it. One won't let you know what's going on with them, while the other is "heart on the sleeve." The high S feels uncomfortable by the displays of affection and the low S feels unnerved by the lack of emotion!

And then the C difference — one the rules-person, the other the rebel shaking things up and questioning everything. The low C sees the high C as "anal-retentive" — worried about everything and focused on doing it right. The high C thinks the low C is irresponsible, a maverick who doesn't care about quality or controls. In an organization, one is perceived to be the rules-enforcer while the other is a rebel, causing problems just for the sake of causing problems.

And so we exist, or coexist, each disliking the other's styles and wondering why everyone can't be like us! Again, it's the labels we assign when someone is different that cause us the problem.

As a boss, or a member of a team, or a partner in a relationship, it's really critical that we see our own style for what it is and observe and respond to the style of others. We want very much to have the other person or people behave just like we do. We think we're the ones who are right, and we don't want to be the ones who have to modify ourselves or our behaviors.

Cheat Sheet on the Styles

We talked earlier about the different styles and how they show themselves by the tone, pace, and type of words that people use. A shorthand way for identifying the different behaviors is as follows (and remember that those who are low on any of the scales will effectively show the opposite reaction!):

- **High D:** fast talking, fast moving, and oriented to tasks. They want to get something done! Give 'em a challenge and let 'em loose!
- **High I:** fast-talking, fast-moving, and oriented to people. Energized and optimistic, they are focused on the experience.
- **High S:** slower-talking, slower-moving, but oriented toward the good of the team. They will accommodate and work tirelessly to get things done — for everyone.
- **High C:** the slowest of all the styles in their thinking and their talking. They are oriented toward the task at hand, and want things to be "right" and will uphold the quality standards and the rules.

The Positive — and the Negative — of Each Style

Each style and each combination has its "good" points and its difficulties. The key is in understanding that when we clash with one another — i.e. my style is too abrasive, too direct, and too fast-moving for yours, or vice versa — we aren't really seeing the difference in styles, we're just seeing the person who annoys us.

The more we can recognize these style differences, and try to match our behavior to that person we are working hard to communicate with, the more we will be understood by the other. It isn't a matter of being "fake," it's a matter of being heard. We simply can't hear when another person is speaking in such a different behavioral manner from the one that we recognize — our own.

Understanding behavioral style and learning how to modify our own approach and the way we interact helps us to open communication with those people with styles very different from our own.

What to Do?

In the consulting work we've done with behavioral style, we've seen how powerful simply understanding this material can be. If you recognized your own behavior and approach, or that of others you interact with, and want to use DISC to communicate more effectively, consider these step-by-step instructions to implement Secret Number Two:

1. Realize that almost every interaction you have where you "click" with someone is because there are probably behavioral similarities between the two of you, and when you "grate" on someone it is usually because you have different styles from one another. Think about those people in your life who, in most interactions, just "irritate" you, and think about whether there is a behavioral disconnect (there usually is!).

2. In your future interactions, listen to tone of voice, watch body language, and so on, and try to slightly "match" the person you are talking with. Observe whether they become more open and friendly toward you when you start communicating as they do. In sales, this is called "mirroring," and it's used because people

tend to like people who are like them and buy from people that
they like.

3.   Remember, we like people who are like us, so I want you to communicate with me the way I like to communicate. It makes it
easier on me if there is recognition of you and your style. Our
communication will be easier and more open if we are naturally
similar to one another. This doesn't happen all of the time, of
course. To be an effective communicator, if you really want to
be heard — you have to be the one to observe and modify. Be
the person who understands the differences and is willing to
make the modifications. You can't wait for the world to be like
you. Your relationships will immediately improve if you start
behaving more like them — so you are able to get through and
communicate more effectively.

People always ask me if I am recommending being "fake" and turning
into something that we're not because I suggest that they change their
style to match that of the other person. I'm not recommending that — in
fact, we can't change our fundamental style in any of the categories.
We can modify and adapt to situations and other people, though. If
you want communication to increase and you want to be understood
(it *is* all about you, isn't it?), then be the one to do the adapting. Communication will naturally be improved as a result and the people you
are interacting with will say, "S/he really understands me!"

Secret Number One:
It's All About ME!

Secret Number Two:
Our Behavioral Styles Come Between Us

Secret Number Three:
Your Values Speak Louder Than You Do

Secret Number Four:
Don't Assume I Know What You Mean

Secret Number Five:
I'm Okay, You Are Most Definitely NOT Okay

Putting It All Together:
What To Do Next

Secret Number Three:
Your Values Speak Louder Than You Do

While behavioral style comes across and can be observed by what we do, values are the why — the reasons for what we do. Values are much more under-the-covers than behavioral style. Behavioral style is observable — I can see how you interact with me, and I can watch your behavior and know how I might need to modify my behavior (or at least why we aren't connecting very well).

Values are more difficult to figure out. We don't necessarily express them in an easy-to-read fashion. However, once you learn Secret Number Three, you'll be able to figure out the values that lie hidden in others and understand that while they aren't as overt as behavior, we do show the world what is important to us. By becoming a keen observer, you'll discover that values are underneath everything we do, and come into play in our daily decisions.

Six Core Values

Edward Spranger's research from the turn of the century, written in his book, "Types of Men," identified six core values: Utilitarian, Individualistic, Theoretical, Social, Aesthetic, and Traditional. For each of us, our values will fall into preferences beginning with number one (our top, and most important value) and descending to number six (our least important and one we may even disdain in others). In terms of relative importance we care about each of the six in one way or another — the ones we have in the first and second position are the most important to us, the middle values we may be indifferent to or care nothing about, and the last two values may be anathema to us.

The conflict arises in the day-to-day situation where *I* have two top values that I consider the most important in all of the decisions I make. *You* have those same two values as your bottom two — the ones you may disdain. You don't agree with my view, don't understand my view, and may not even like me because I'm espousing a value structure that is opposite to the one that you believe in. Let's look at each of the values and see how they drive our decision-making.

Utilitarian: Driven by ROI and Maximizing Value

Utilitarian, value-driven people are focused on their Return on Investment (ROI). They want to gain a return on any investment of time, money, and energy. This often manifests itself in tangible profit, like starting up a successful company or investing in a new idea, but it can control even day-to-day decisions like shopping at the supermarket.

A high Utilitarian person would never go to the store for just one item (unless it was a very valuable item to them). They would instead go with a list of ten things they needed. If they were to get nine of them, run into an old friend and chat, then forget to get the tenth thing but remember it on the way home, they would most likely not turn the car around to go back and get that tenth thing (unless it was the one key ingredient they needed for their recipe!). It's all about maximizing time and gaining the best return.

As an example from a client situation of ours, the person in charge who is High Utilitarian is going to ask specifically how we can measure success and know that the investment they've made in us is paying off for them. That's a classic Utilitarian approach to life.

We often see the leaders, or senior management, of a firm with Utilitarian as their number one value. It indicates a need for tangible return on an investment, so the people with this value often gravitate to roles where they can truly make, and measure, an impact. These are people who would care about the profit equation on a decision they are trying to make — they might ask, "Will this yield me a profitable return for the time and money I expect to spend?" Every decision, for a person with a Utilitarian approach, will be viewed through a lens of what the payoff might be for taking that next step.

Individualistic: Driven by Ego

Individualistic, value-driven people have a focus on ego-oriented activities. The scale used to be called "Political," because many politicians who like to be in the limelight are high on the Individualistic value. People with this value like to see their name in lights. They like to be successful and commended for their personal contributions. It's very important for the person with this value to be recognized publicly for their achievements.

People who are strong on the D category in the DISC measurement and high in the Individualistic value will often come across as ego-centric — they are hard drivers who are looking for recognition for their achievements. It's an important value for them to be known and seen as a player and contributor — someone really making a difference and being recognized for it.

As such, they may be labeled as the "blowhard" or the guy (or gal) in charge who "thinks they are so great." A client example here is the person in charge of the firm who, every time a memo goes out, thinks about what the staff is going to think of him.

In one case, we had a longstanding client of ours who needed to send out information via e-mail to his co-workers. However, the new information slightly contradicted something the head of the firm had sent the day before and he felt that while necessary, it would make him "look bad," so he didn't send it.

Quite often leaders will match Individualistic with Utilitarian. If we remember that Utilitarian folks are focused on a return on investment (ROI) and Individualistic can appear as "ego-centered" with a focus on how they are personally doing and being perceived — this combination comes across as the desire to reap a tangible reward for what you've done, and to have your name associated with that success!

Theoretical: A Lifelong Love of Learning

Theoretical, value-driven people love to learn. They are lifelong learners, and to them the world is just one big classroom where ideas and new experiences abound. Theoreticals will often be found reading five books at one time — usually on five different topics, or the same topics they enjoy. They'll take every seminar and class that comes along, then go home and read everything they can find on the subject. They typically like to find jobs and companies where people are smart and the work is challenging and engaging. They want to be around smart people and in a stimulating environment where they can continue to learn and be challenged by new learning experiences.

Our client example here is the very successful accountant who went home at night and watched the Discovery Channel because of a high Theoretical need to learn something new every day. Theoreticals need to be careful because they can spend too much time in learning mode gaining knowledge, and not enough time doing something with the knowledge that they've gained! Often they will end up in teaching or researching roles, where gaining knowledge is central to their day-to-day activities.

We have a client who performs a behavioral profile (the DISC) and a values profile on every new hire. Making sure that someone is a cultural fit (the values) is very important to this successful, small firm. Because the work they do is very challenging, and very cutting edge, they tend to attract high Theoretical values. It works well because everyone in the environment is smart and thrives on being around other smart people. In their case, the firm's values are a combination of the Theoretical with Utilitarian, so these smart people are seeking the best way to make a lot of money for what they know how to do!

Social: Doing Good for Others

Social, value-driven people are motivated by others — they focus on other people. Often they want to make a contribution, so they will invest time in charitable endeavors or spend time where they are able to interact with people. Social-driven managers will frequently make decisions that focus on "How will this impact our people and our customers?" It's an "other" focus on the world, with little to no focus on helping "me." Keep in mind there is an element of self-perception where they may want to view themselves as giving, loving, and caring about other people. If the strong social value doesn't manifest in "doing good", it may show itself as being focused on relationships and being in relationship with others.

The example for Social is the client we worked with that was hiring a high Social person to their staff. That person wanted to interview with every single member of the firm to ensure the "fit" was there. This is classic Social being played out in the interview process.

In one client situation we had a group of five managers, four of which had Utilitarian in the number one category and one who scored the highest on Social. In every decision they would make, the four would agree together from a "profit" perspective, but the fifth manager, the one with the Social value, always felt that there was simply no attention or care being given to the impact on employees, clients, and the world at large. No matter how often they discussed decisions, they could never see eye to eye.

It illustrated how hard it is for groups of people in a team environment with differing value structures to reach decisions that everyone can feel good about. Fundamentally, if we differ in our value views, the decisions we make (compromise in some cases) won't make both of us happy. We see the criteria for what's important as completely different. So those people, for example, with a strong Social value will often believe that others making a decision for any other reason, or value, simply "don't care" about the potential impact on others.

Traditional: The "Right Way" to do Things

The Traditional value used to be termed "Religious," because frequently it is a set of religious values gained from association with a specific religion. Traditional, value-driven people believe that a given set of rules exists and that they — and others — should abide by those rules because they are critically important. Traditional values can also be "family values" or doing things in "traditional" cultural ways. Traditional value people may be viewed as the "Bible-thumping" individuals at corporate meetings, or may spend their weekends and down-time at retreats with other members of their faith.

A high Traditional client of ours insisted that all staff members bring their families to a company event. Those who refused or were unable to make it were looked down upon and ostracized by the person in charge. Another high Traditional client held Bible study meetings and expected staff members to attend, even though the business they were in had nothing to do with any religious leaning or affiliation.

A person who has a strong Traditional value can sometimes come across as pushing the "right or wrong" way to deal with life because of their belief system. They focus on upholding the rules and guidelines that they believe to be important. They can strongly express their religious or lifestyle viewpoints to someone else and appear judgmental in their quest to get others to understand their highest value or they may just quietly hold their beliefs and follow them. Having something to believe in and a guidebook to follow is very important to the person with the high Traditional value.

Aesthetic: Looking for Beauty in the World

Aesthetic, value-driven people look for beauty in the world. They are interested in, and focused on, beautiful things. The cubicle they are in is likely decorated nicely, their clothes always match perfectly and are ironed "just so," and they need to be around beautiful things. A person with a high Aesthetic value would notice and care about the color of the walls where they work and the opportunity to get outside into nature or into beautiful surroundings.

A client we worked with whose company was in some financial trouble went out and bought all new furniture and beautiful purple rugs. When we went in to have a meeting about the financial situation and what to do next, he wanted to talk about the Art Deco furniture — not what he needed to do to save the company! It was very important to him to be surrounded by beautiful things and have an area he felt good working in. It simply didn't matter that there were financial constraints and perhaps he "should not have" spent the money.

This is a perfect example of where values override what, to someone else, may appear to be a "logical" decision not to spend money unnecessarily.

Understanding the Other Viewpoint

The values can wreak havoc in the following ways — if you and I are trying to make a decision together regarding what to do about something, I am focused on my top two values, while you are focused on your top two. If we share values, no problem; we "see eye to eye." If we don't...well, that's when the fun starts. If there's a decision that has to be made between three people with different values in the number one position, let's consider what might happen. The Utilitarian person, for example, may focus solely on the money being spent and whether whatever we're deciding to do is "worth it." The Social person in the group doesn't care much about the money but rather whether it is a good decision for the people involved and if everyone will be well taken care of. The Aesthetic person is looking around the room thinking, "I can't focus on decisions about the budget right now or who we help, we need to redecorate around here; these these shabby walls are distracting and depressing to me!"

Values are probably at play in marriages when difficulties arise because of financial issues. A Utilitarian spouse with a non-Utilitarian partner is never going to be able to convince the other that money and ROI matter as much as they believe they do. A Traditional spouse with a non-Traditional partner will never convince the other that "playing by religious rules" is the key to happiness, and so on and so on.

Values in the Filter

Values are entrenched — they are stuck in our filters and we can't remove them. What we can do is recognize that our personal values aren't necessarily the only viewpoint. I don't have to sacrifice my belief in them, or their importance in my life, but I do have to recognize that not everyone shares them.

Back to something we talked about at the opening of this book — we all too often don't want to acknowledge differences; we only want to spend our time trying to convince the other person that we're "right." Well, guess what, that other person *is* wrong — in your eyes and in your value system. But before you go running off to tell your spouse that I said they were wrong, remember that *you* are wrong — to your spouse.

We can't bring another person around to our way of thinking on values. We just can't. We can help them understand why they matter to us and we may learn to live peaceably accepting the differences, but they will remain there. It's the effort we put into trying to convince the other person to see the world through our set of values (and in turn, our filter) that really causes us the problem. The old adage of "live and let live" applies here somewhat. Why can't I rest knowing that you have the values you do — if they differ from my own? Instead, I try to make you "change your mind" so that you value what I do.

Values are very powerful in any situation where you have to make decisions in concert with another person, or other people. We have another client who runs the DISC (behavioral) profile and values profile for every new candidate to their firm. They also have a certain culture where everyone in a leadership role shares the same top two values. This firm hired a candidate who did not have these two values, but with whom the leader of the firm felt comfortable because of an existing relationship with this candidate. Fast-forward to a few months later when this new person was working with the firm — and they were trying to figure out how best to fire him!

Was he a bad employee or incompetent at what he did? No. Was he totally out of sync with the rest of management on what really mattered to the firm? Yes. Values create schisms with people and when we're forced to confront one another, we'll rebel against those people who share a different view on what's important in the world from the one we may share. We do this completely without knowing that the underlying reason we can't see eye-to-eye is that our values are in conflict. It's Secret Number Three — I know something is at odds between how I view a decision being made, and how you may view it. The problem is that I don't understand what's amiss. What I do recognize is that our differences seem to speak very loudly. The differences are clear, but without understanding the existence of values, I may judge you — and you may judge me.

What to Do? Love Your Values — and Leave Others Alone

What to do about differing values? Remember that you can't change another's mind. What you can do is acknowledge the existence of the six values and pay close attention to find where they show themselves in relationships with others. Here's how to employ the Secret Number Three, step by step:

1. Using the knowledge that not everyone shares the same values that you do — when you get into an argument with someone and find yourself wanting to "change their mind" or bring them around to your way of thinking — just drop it. Drop your need to be right. Drop your need to convince others that what you believe is important. It's freeing to recognize that I can have my values, live my values, and make decisions by my values, and you don't have to share them. And anyway, if we all held the same values, the world really would get pretty boring. Enjoy the values you care about — find ways to nurture them and attend to them.

2. Recognize the labels you put on people when their values conflict with yours. Married to someone who doesn't care much about money, but you are a "high Utilitarian?" Frustrated by their seeming lack of care and concern about money? It's time to understand that it's a value mismatch. What matters to you, simply doesn't matter to them. Find a way to understand it and live with it instead of gnashing your teeth and yelling at them to change to your way of thinking. Realize that there is a values mismatch and try to accept that some decisions they make, while you may not completely agree with them, were the right decisions for that person, in their values framework.

3. Watch yourself and your day-to-day decisions. Spend more time looking inward and questioning why others' viewpoints set you off or upset you, and less time criticizing what everyone else is doing, because the values aren't the same for everyone.

4. Listen when others talk to you about what matters, or give the basis for a decision they are making. You will often find — if you listen — that you can hear the underlying values that they care about coming through in what they say. Learning the values of another, and respecting them, helps you to make better decisions because you've learned to incorporate other's values. The more you can uncover the values of the other person, the more influence you are able to exert over the decisions that get made.

Secret Number Four:
Don't Assume I Know What You Mean

Secret Number Four is really all about context and using your understanding that other people are not you, and then using this information to allow you to become a more successful communicator. If you've accepted so far that it's all about *me*, and you've come to recognize the behavioral differences between us, and you've understood that values speak very loudly — you can see that we initially approach other people assuming that they have the same perspective that we do. We share what we want to share and expect someone else to completely understand all of our context and meaning. But don't assume I know what you mean, because I don't. I haven't walked in your shoes, lived your life, had your experiences, and come to the same conclusions you've come to. And, most importantly, I can't read your mind, and you can't read mine, so we don't have the ability to see clearly all of what's underlying our communication.

Let Others In

The fourth secret has to do with our unwillingness, or inability, to share enough information to be candid about ourselves to give another person a true opportunity to hear us and to understand what we are trying to express. How many times have you said to yourself, or another person, "He/She just doesn't understand me?" Well, understand this—they can't, unless you are willing to take the time to help them. Their filters are busy being clogged with *their* experiences, background, thoughts, feelings, etc. And unless they've read this book and understand the Five Secrets, they can't put all of what matters to them to the side and understand you and what you're trying to communicate. Combine this fact with the idea that generally when we do express communication, we don't give enough information to help someone to fully "hear" what we're trying to say.

We give just a little bit to those people around us, and we expect it to be enough. Best of all, we share ourselves using our communication styles (behavioral and DISC preferences), our underlying values (one of the top two or three that matter to us), and with our filters completely intact.

If I'm like you, and have lived through similar experiences and communicate in a similar fashion, I may be able to get into your shoes for a bit (which is again why some of us love our long-time friends!), but chances are good that we've not shared everything alike. As we noted, even your sibling with the same parents, the same home, and the same experiences didn't turn out like you did and may not see the world the same way you do.

The problem is, without some background provided along with an understanding of why the information should matter to me—including how I should understand it, why it matters to me, and what I should do with it—I don't have a way to integrate it into my existing understanding. It's about context—giving me enough information so that I am able to get a window into what you mean, and why it matters.

Define Your Own Success

Many times when my consulting firm has an assignment, the client will ask us to do a particular type of work. They may say, "We want to increase revenue next year and we want your help with a new marketing program." My first response is always to ask what success looks like to them. If I assume I know what they mean by "increasing revenue" or "new marketing program" based upon my filters, my viewpoint, and my past experiences, then I will run off and start to put a program in place based upon what I care about and I believe is most important. In order for me to be successful in my role, I need to know what they believe is most important.

When we ask the success question, we get as many different definitions of success as numbers of people we've worked with. Once in a while, someone will respond and say, "That's a good question! I hadn't thought of the answer to that one." Well, if they don't have a clear success definition, how in the world am I ever going to be able to offer a solution that meets their needs?

Each firm and each individual person defines what they are seeking differently — and what they need in order to feel "successful" at the end. If I don't know — at the outset — what the client defines as success, I'm going to have to work very hard and cross my fingers all along the way that I'm striving for the same outcome that they are paying me to strive for! It's a risky proposition on both of our parts to assume anything. We need to devote energy to being clear about what we really mean underneath the words we use with one another.

This gets compounded by the perception, in the work I do, that consultants don't know much and charge too much for their services. If I encounter a client who has this filter (unbeknownst to me, of course) and I don't clarify right in the beginning what they need, and how they define success, aren't I destined to fail with their assignment? They expect me, as a consultant, to offer something less valuable than what they are paying for. If we aren't both clear, right up front, what the end goal really looks like, I could believe I've done a great job for their company, and they could believe I "robbed them" because it didn't turn out as they'd expected.

Knowing What Matters to Me

This point is equally relevant in the individual setting when I work with hypnosis clients. In hypnosis we do something called an "induction" where we use words and imagery for the client to reach a state where they are open to suggestions. There are scripts and standard inductions that one can learn and use with clients. The fact of "don't assume I know what you mean" can be critically important here.

If you use a word, for example, that the client doesn't understand, or imagery that they can't relate to, you'll be unsuccessful in gaining their trust and finding them to be open to the process. I once learned this the hard way when I used imagery about the beach (calming and positive for me) and later learned that the client had been attacked by a dog on the beach and was deathly afraid of ever going there again! The experience taught me that I have to understand the client's words, likes, dislikes, and what matters to them before I can be helpful meeting their needs.

Hey, Stop Yelling at Me!

Watching this dynamic in action shows us how we can feel so misunderstood, or can really misunderstand other people. How does this work in our personal interactions? A recent personal example from my own life illustrates the power of Secret Number Four.

I had an incident with an organization that rescues dogs. I have adopted three, fostered two, and am considering adopting my fourth. Everyone I've dealt with over the years in the animal rescue community is so dedicated (my label and my filter). But the other day I received a call from my adoption coordinator (the third one I've had) to talk about the dog I am currently fostering. She called to tell me about an application in for this dog. She didn't have the information she needed to have about the dog, so I shared information that I had and that, obviously (as I learned later), she was supposed to have had, but the organization hadn't passed along to her.

I thought I was being "helpful" (my label) and sharing information that would be of benefit to her, so I readily opened up and told her everything I knew about this dog. But I made the mistake of assuming she had a similar understanding and background about the whole situation (with me and the dog) and would know what I meant and understand my intentions.

I blindly thought if I shared this information, she would be able to respond to me in a way that I anticipated (in other words, I assumed she would know what I meant!). Instead, after I'd shared what I knew, she started to verbally attack me and used the information I had given her as fodder for an attack on my approach, and my behavior as a foster-mom — telling me all of the things I'd done wrong, how I needed to communicate better with her, and so on.

How quickly my experience changed — I went from feeling like the "do-gooder" helpful foster-mom, to the bad woman who had information that she shouldn't have and who hadn't taken the right steps to care for this poor dog! Honestly, because I wasn't feeling well, I was so distressed at being yelled at for having done nothing wrong (in my viewpoint, through my filter) that I thought I might cry when I hung up the phone, and I am not a crier!

I found out later on that the organization had recently had an unfortunate experience with a foster situation that had turned out badly for everyone concerned. Somehow my comments reminded her of this other situation and she "replaced" me with the other foster family (her filter, and her expectation). Another woman from the organization, whom I have a good relationship with and respect, called me to apologize and explain everything.

The funny thing is — it didn't matter. I realize the original caller replaced me in her mind with someone who had committed a "wrong," but she didn't take two minutes to "walk in my shoes" — to "seek to understand." She assumed I knew what she meant and what mattered to her, and quite honestly, I assumed she would know what I meant and why I was sharing the information I was. My experience was so reactive that I didn't take the time to step outside our interaction, and try and understand why she would be so mad at me — someone she doesn't even know. Both of us assumed, and neither of us understood.

Seek to Understand: Don't Assume

This is an excellent example of how we pass one another without really seeing our interactions. Neither of us knew, or took the time to consider, the context of the other person. She thought she "knew me" and launched into an attack on me (my filter and experience!). Even as the incident was unfolding, I realized the whole time that she wasn't really yelling at *me*, but even knowing these secrets, it still upset me that I was being used in place of someone else.

She assumed something about me, and something about what I was doing. And because I value my strong communication skills and my commitment to the animal rescue community, too, it really bothered me that she didn't understand me! Her approach to me implied that I wasn't doing very well with either of these two areas that really matter to me (communicating about my fostered dog and caring about the rescue efforts). We didn't have enough information about one another or about why we were exchanging the information we were. We just made our assumptions and dug in our heels.

Think about it — we do this all the time. I'm mad at myself, or my spouse, or my boss, and then you walk into the room. You say one thing that sets me off (a "trigger") and all of a sudden I'm replacing that other person with your body! All of a sudden you're thinking (as I was on the phone), "Why is he/she yelling at *me*?"

To put this idea in perspective, think whether you've ever had a spouse or significant other or member of your family, for example, say in some frustration, "Well, I can't read your mind!" And the truth is that they can't — but we want them to, and even worse, we expect them to. Then we'll get frustrated on our end if they don't. I want you to automatically understand that I've had a bad day, or I don't feel well, or I'm struggling with something and want you immediately to come to my aid, or my conclusion, or my way of thinking. Only — I'm not giving you the chance.

You don't know everything about me, but I won't give up my hope that you will understand me fully and know me deeply. But it's really asking too much of another person (with their filters, styles, etc. in place) to be *me*! It's never going to happen. With all of the clogged filters and different approaches walking around, some days I can't read my *own* mind, never mind yours!

Help Me to Understand You

In our communication efforts with everyone we come into contact with, we need to become aware of how little time we really take to understand the other person if we want to open our communication. We can't assume that they know what we mean. We have to own the responsibility of explaining our needs, our thoughts, and our concerns, and making sure they are conveyed in a way that the listener can follow. The difficult part is that we have to do all of this while we carefully place *me* aside to focus on communicating with the other person.

How could this all work differently for a different outcome? Let's replay the phone call. If the woman calling me understood the fourth of the Five Secrets, she would explain that my information was news to her. That she had a bad experience with another foster and was feeling "put off" by my news. She would ask me more questions to understand what I was really telling her about the situation. She would not assume that I knew what she meant! By assuming, she went on the offensive with me. Because I didn't know what *she* meant, I felt defensive about it. I would then also recognize that there must be something underlying her outrage at me — I would also seek to understand and not make assumptions that "she's just a jerk." I would put aside my own filters (they freeze up every time someone yells at me without what I think is just cause), and I would drop my labels and practice listening without my voices talking in my head about her.

What happened instead was two people, both assuming that the other one knew what they meant and what they needed to know, but neither person fully understanding or communicating well at all. And as a result both people were left with bad feelings, even though both started with good intentions.

That's the most difficult outcome of Secret Number Four — when we don't know it, don't understand it, and don't work with it. We may have the best of intentions as we approach others and interact with others. But if we don't take the time to help them understand what we mean, and we don't provide the context to someone else about what we know, why it matters, and what we expect from them, we'll be continually frustrated by the lack of responsiveness on the part of others with whom we are communicating.

Clear — or Cloudy?

It's a vicious cycle without an end when we blindly go through life and just assume that the other person understands. Ever had a situation, perhaps in a dating scenario or with a boss or co-worker, where you were just certain that you had been clear in your communication but then something happens and you can't believe how "off" you were? The other person clearly didn't understand, or understood something entirely different from what you were trying to communicate? And this is how it goes — and goes — and goes. In fact, we build off of this — your assumption about me and then my assumption about you. It's a wonder we ever get through to one another! But we can, and we do — when we are willing to stop and really put a focus on the other person. If we make it our goal to use communication as a teaching tool with others, we'll find ourselves taking the time to communicate more fully and more completely.

What do I mean by "teaching tool"? With children in grade school and middle school, I see many concepts and ideas that I've forgotten about from my past schooling. The way they are taught isn't as if they should already know everything. In other words, they are given background, context, and a thorough explanation of anything that is a new subject. What if we, in our daily interactions, approached others like this? What if we didn't make any assumptions that the information we need to share, or the communication we're trying to have, is automatically understood? What if we approached it as if we have a responsibility to "teach" someone else what we want them to know?

Drop Your Assumptions

To do this, we have to keep practicing the art of dropping our assumptions, and in particular dropping our need to be the one who is "right." Instead, we need to set a priority on really learning about others and wanting to understand what they mean, and how they feel. If we can ask ourselves what we're hearing, what the other person is really saying, and find out what they are thinking about (and pay attention to what we are thinking about while they are talking!), we start to have the "Aha!" of understanding.

When we say to someone, "I think I am understanding what you are trying to communicate," we'll really mean it. We'll really have the context and the understanding to get a window into what they are talking about and why it matters. Without the context, and when we just assume that others know what we mean, we're spending our time conversing and "communicating" with no real understanding about what the communication is really all about!

Understanding Secret Number Four really requires quite a bit of effort on each of our parts. If you can't — and don't — assume I know what you mean, it puts a great deal more responsibility on you to ensure you take the time, and the care, to help me understand. You'll do whatever you can to ensure my understanding because you want us to have a true connection. When we behave this way, communication becomes a more complicated process because I have to stop and consider whether you really understand me, and whether I understand you. It raises the ante on each interaction. It's so much easier to get annoyed with you, or frustrated by the exchange we've had, or ignore you altogether.

In our quest for true communication, we do have to really work at it. Many people will say, "If I have to both share something of myself and put in the effort to share the context and background and 'teach' you about my viewpoint, I may as well not bother talking!" But in fact, if we don't do this each time, we really aren't communicating — so although we may have spent less time and energy, our results and our connection with the other person are much less also.

Don't Just Dump on Others

If we think about the many different interactions we have with others each day, we'll notice there are times we only have the goal to dump our ideas or our experience on someone else. We just want to express ourselves! We aren't really looking for an interaction with the other person; we just want to share something because it matters to *us*. But it's useless sharing if I don't also take the time to make sure I've shared enough so that I give you the chance to understand what I really mean. Only in doing so can I open communication with you, have you understand me, and begin a meaningful dialogue.

Once you've understood all of the secrets leading up to this one, the fourth secret is really pretty clear. When we communicate with someone, it goes something like this: I have my idea about what I want you to know or think or understand. Instead of thinking about it from your perspective, I think about how I need to get this information across, with my style, my values, my agenda intact.

There is a saying in sales about everyone's favorite radio station — WIIFM (What's in it for me?). In teaching salespeople, as I've done for almost 20 years, I try to help them to understand that thinking about what they are saying from the other person's perspective is key. In the sales example, the prospect knows that you want to sell them something, so it's really on you — as a salesperson — to work at putting whatever you are selling into a frame that matters to that person. It's just *so* hard…and why? Because we like to assume that the other person we're communicating with already knows what we know, and so we'll share our information from our experience, not from theirs.

In the salesperson example, the salesperson knows their product and their service and they know they need to sell it. It is how they get paid, after all. Whether you, as the prospect, want to buy it, or even "need" it can become irrelevant. The salesperson needs to sell it — period. Some won't worry about taking the time to understand your situation. Of course, the best salespeople do take the time to understand whether what they are selling is really right for the person they hope will buy it.

Put it in Context

I call this dilemma of wanting to communicate, but not taking the time to do so, a "context" problem, which is that I don't stop and take the time to explain to you the meaning behind what I'm saying. In the sales arena there are many books written on the art of consultative selling and the art of asking questions. Why? Because, as we've just discussed, so many salespeople are just focused on what they need to sell (it *is* all about them, isn't it?) and don't take the time to put what they have to offer in a framework that lets the person on the other side of the desk say, "I see how this matters to me."

Remember how we talked about the product or service that would change my life and my willingness to embrace it if it resonated with me? Again, good marketers have assumed certain things about certain segments of the population — what baby boomers care about, what tweens care about, and what women might care about, for example. And in many cases, they are right about some of the themes — they've assumed correctly.

This is the idea behind mass marketing. But in a one-to-one exchange, most people won't buy unless they have been shown how the "offer" fits their specific life and needs. Salespeople who take the time to learn about what matters to their prospect or customer, and who don't assume the prospect knows what they mean, will always be more successful.

It's a common dynamic we observe that many people, when trying to sway someone else to their point of view, will embark on the "data dump" approach to communicating. This means that I show up and give you every piece of data and information I can relative to my own viewpoint. I don't stop and make any connection for you. I don't try and link the information to anything that matters to you, I just assume you know what I mean and, if you don't, well — that's your problem!

So our frustration rises because we've given everything we have, and the other person still doesn't understand. Adult learning principles tell us that adults need to learn new information in a context of something they already understand — something that matters to them. So if I want you to understand — I need to take the time to make sure I am communicating in a way, and with a style, that both makes sense, and matters, to you.

Say That Again?

Have you ever had an experience in which you have an exchange with someone that seemed innocent and nonthreatening to you, but they got upset or angry at you about it? Obviously something hasn't gone well in the exchange and there is a misunderstanding or conflict. But then, after you each have had some time to cool off, or had some time to think, you go back and talk to the person again because you sincerely want them to understand.

You really want to get your side of the story across and communicate your position, so the second time you may use different language or a different emotional approach. All of a sudden you see the light go on with the other person and they say, "*That's* what you have been talking about? Why didn't you just *say so* in the first place?"

Even as I write this, I have to laugh. It's the fourth secret; I assume you know all along what I am trying to communicate, and only when something goes drastically wrong in our exchange will I take the time, or make the effort, to help you to understand. Once I do that, you may actually be able to see it from my perspective. Think about the time we'd save if I understood the fourth secret and set out in the conversation to help you to understand in the first place.

While I was writing this, I took an incoming call from a potential client. She was seeking help but wasn't really sure how to convey what she needed, so she began talking to me in very general terms and being very unclear about her needs. It took me about 25 minutes of unpaid time to talk with her and ask her questions to try to really understand what she wanted to accomplish.

Once I learned what she was seeking, I realized there was no way we could help her with her needs. But, at the end of our conversation, she thanked me profusely for taking the time to try to understand and help her to clarify what she wanted. Again, it made me laugh. How could I help if I don't really know what she's talking about? And without taking the time, how could I know? But we typically hear a piece of what we *do* understand and what fits into our own set of filters, and then we launch into a response based upon what we know.

If I had only listened to a part of her dilemma, I would have started to pitch her on one of our services that seemed to fit what she was telling me. If I had done this, it would be very low-priced work for us and not necessarily that useful to her or her firm. Was it worth my time to talk with her, listen, and give her feedback, when I was never going to stand a chance of getting paid for doing so? For me, yes — I was creating a reputation in a very small industry as someone who will take the time to listen. It may not pay off for me right now, but the longer-term reputation of being someone who understands is invaluable.

Be Jealous of Your Attention

Many times we simply feel that we don't have time in the day to be a "good listener" and to work to understand others. It's one of the reasons why, over time, we need to become somewhat jealous about where we do spend our time and attention. Each exchange with someone else does require focus and attention. Some days we just don't have as much as we need — and as much as will serve us well. We can be so distracted by the many issues in our day and with the things we are trying to give our mindshare to that we sometimes can't really stop and put a complete focus on another person.

But taking the time to understand, to listen and engage, and to use our best active listening skills, and all the while dropping our need to be the one who does understand, serves us well in all interactions. On the other side of the equation, taking time to really think about what we want to say and communicate to someone else in a clear manner, and checking to make sure they have really heard what we are saying, makes us better communicators. It gives us more assurance that we will get our needs met and engage in dialogue that works for both parties. Going into every exchange refusing to assume that the other person will know what we mean is a good place to start working toward more effective communication.

The key piece of Secret Number Four is that we really have to want to be understood by others, and we have to want to understand others. It's honestly much easier to just put my info and my data out there into the universe and feel good about having done that. In other words, what matters to me is the fact that I've shared something of myself, and not really whether or not anyone else has understood me. And if we make this choice, we confine ourselves to sitting in our *own* little universe without much real interaction with others. For some people, that's what they want (their filters) but others truly want to connect. In order to connect, we have to understand that others don't know what we mean most of the time. The commitment to help them understand — coupled with the commitment to really learn what happens within another person — takes work. But, it's worth it when we start to really open up communication — and feel as though we are being heard, and hearing others.

What to Do? Cease to Assume

Here are some ideas for a step-by-step implementation for Secret Number Four:

1. The easiest way to conserve energy and to invest the time where it really matters is to save your interactions with people for those you really care about. Once the meaning of this fourth secret really settles in, some people find that "making small talk" is no longer interesting or important to them. Engaging with people

when you really don't care how it turns out seems nonsensical when you think about the energy involved in getting others to really understand what you mean. You have to share enough to make it meaningful for someone else — and you have to be willing to listen to others share enough to make it meaningful for them.

2. When you do interact — put your all into it. Turn into a communication detective, and really try and understand what the other person is communicating to you. Listen for understanding, and don't stop until you feel you have a window into what the other person is trying to communicate to you and why. When you want to get something across, take the time to help the other person understand what you mean. Give them context and background — be the "teacher." Not in a patronizing way, like: "Let me teach *you* something," but rather in a way that shares enough information so that the person you're talking to has a chance to really learn something new about you.

3. Commit to "never assume" again that someone else will understand what you mean without your taking the painstaking time to help them understand. No shorthand. No clipped phrases or strangely worded e-mails, just an investment in your time and the other person's time to make sure that communication is flowing. Put information in the context of what matters to the other person, and not just what matters to you.

Secret Number One:
It's All About ME!

Secret Number Two:
Our Behavioral Styles Come Between Us

Secret Number Three:
Your Values Speak Louder Than You Do

Secret Number Four:
Don't Assume I Know What You Mean

Secret Number Five:
I'm Okay, You Are Most Definitely NOT Okay

Putting It All Together:
What To Do Next

Secret Number Five:
I'm Okay; You Are Most Definitely NOT Okay

Do you remember this book from the late '60s: "I'm Okay, You're Okay" by Thomas Harris? In concept, it was a great idea about liking yourself and liking others. Most religions honor the core idea of "loving your neighbor as yourself," so it certainly makes sense at first glance. Unfortunately, in practice we don't really act this way. Deep down we like to believe that we're right, we're the understanding one, we're the one who can communicate — and that everyone else is the problem. If only I could get you to see my viewpoint, and understand that *I'm* right, all would be well with the world. What we really want is a secret key that will enable us to show other people around us that they've been doing it wrong all along and we can help them to do a better job. We all know that the other person over there with whom we hope to communicate is not okay!

After you've taken the time to understand and practice using some of the previous four secrets, I hope you can see the foolishness of the belief that everyone else is wrong and you need to show them the light. The truth is that you, that other person over there, are never going to be "okay" with me because you're not me. You don't talk like me, you don't have the exact same behavioral style I have, or share my values, etc. We seek a reflection of ourselves, someone who will make it easy for us to connect and communicate. Research shows, over and over again, that we will buy from someone we like. *Who* do we like the most? You got it; the person who is most like me! But even if you share a lot of my same characteristics, there will come the day when you annoy me because you aren't exactly — can't be, in fact — like me. You'll never be completely "okay" in my book because you aren't me in the mirror.

Opposites Attract — and Repel

Of course, often in our personal lives, we'll tend to gravitate to someone who is unlike us; the person who can fill the missing part of ourselves — the one we can learn from, or who can cover the areas that we don't excel in. The truth is that, for many couples and partners, over time the differences create a wedge and draw us further apart. If we are aware and can value the differences, and learn from one another, it may work out fine. But if we are unwilling to take the time, and make the energy, to connect with someone who doesn't naturally act, think, or talk like us, we'll find ourselves continually disappointed in our inter-personal interactions. All most people want is to be understood — and to be listened to and valued. If I fundamentally disagree with you, and devalue you because you're different, over time you won't much want to spend time with me. We like to feel validated and valued, not put-down and dismissed.

The irony of this secret, for so many people, is that deep down I don't really feel I am very good. I don't have a strong internal core and good feeling about myself.

You're Reflecting Back — Me!

Outside I project confidence and a sense of righteousness, but inside I may be afraid of being revealed as an impostor! We take our cues oft-times from others' reactions to us. As you've seen by reading these se-crets, others' reactions aren't very credible — not that they intentionally are being dishonest; they just have their filters and behavioral styles, etc. getting in the way of any reaction. The old saying that when you point your finger at someone else in blame or accusation, four fingers are pointing back at you, has meaning. We do see our own reflection in others and it's the main reason certain traits in other people really set us off — push our buttons. Most of the time, if we're honest, it's because the traits we rail against and dislike in others are the same traits that we dislike about ourselves, and may try to keep buried and secret from the rest of the world.

Because of all of the secrets leading up to this fifth one, you know now that most people go through life thinking they are right and expressing it outwardly. They may express that they are the only ones that know what to do and they see things more clearly than others — hey, don't most of us go through life like this? But we're back to our original problem as outlined in the first secret. Deep down I don't want everyone to be like me — I don't even believe *I am okay!* So, isn't it natural I would find you wanting? Growing up and reading the Bible, I always read about loving your neighbor as yourself. I used to ponder this. Doesn't it sound self-serving and self-focused? I used to interpret this as my need to fall in love with myself before I could love anyone else. Seemed like such an ego-centered (my label) command! No, what it's really saying is that we have to gain that inner peace, that inner confidence that we're really okay right where we are and that you are okay right where you are. I can't ever extend the best of me to you, until I am in touch with me and have somehow managed to find peace with what I am in touch with inside of myself.

You Can't Change Anyone Else

In my "Dealing with Difficult People" class, at the opening of the class, I say there is just one important thing I want them to take away from the weeks we are together — that they can't change anyone else. Most people come into a class like this one and want to find the key, the secret to changing the difficult people around them for the better. You can change yourself and your reactions to others — and in turn that may (and usually will) force them to change their reactions, but you can't set out to "fix someone" or scream, cajole, plead, or beg them into changing.

In fact, it's a natural law that the more we push on something the more it will push back on us. So in my efforts to "change" you into what I want you to be, you'll just naturally resist being changed. Think of how this works anytime you've really wanted to see different behavior from someone you care about. Anyone else have a parent who smoked when you were growing up? We wasted an awful lot of energy trying to get my dad to "see the light" and stop with his 4-5 packs a day habit. It frustrated us, for sure, and it didn't change him! Only when he decided it was time to stop, did he stop — years after we'd given up on trying to change him!

How much of our lives are spent trying to change the people "out there" — the difficult people getting in *our* way? We waste time and energy trying to fix everyone else, instead of spending that energy finding our own inner calm confidence and being secure with who we are. Only when I am secure in my own being can I welcome you in and let you be who you are.

An interesting story from teaching my graduate class illustrates this well: I had one student in my class who was adamant that we *can* change others. It was evidently extremely frustrating to him, given that his expressed desire of the class was to learn how to change the people who were getting in his way. I kept reiterating my mantra that we can't change others. We talked about coping strategies and ways to modify our own responses, but I never wavered in my insistence that the class would not learn how to change "those out there."

At the end of the semester, the University has all teachers and classes rated without the teacher in the room, so my class students rated their experience and their professor. When the tabulated results came in, all of the students (except one) gave me rave reviews — "Hire this teacher full-time," "Make this a mandatory course," etc. One student wrote, "This teacher never starts class on time. She needs to stop students from talking." Now I have no way to really know who wrote this, and I don't want to waste the time wondering about it, but I certainly have my suspicions about the one person it could be.

Maybe I'm wrong, but just having the experience illustrated for me — again — how our filters, our styles, our beliefs, and our feelings about what's "okay" and what's not, really control us. The irony for me — my filter — that kicked in, is that I'm very "time focused" — I like to get places on time, so even though I didn't even think it was really true, I had a negative reaction and felt accused that someone believed I wouldn't start a class on time.

I'm Really Okay?

The fifth secret is one that once mastered brings a certain level of peace into one's life. If I can somehow allow myself to believe that I'm doing my best and I'm really okay where I am right now, and you are okay where you are, then we have nothing to fight about, do we? It doesn't mean I stop trying to improve myself and my approach to others — that's why you are reading this book, isn't it? It's just that I start to give myself a break that I'm not perfect and I can't expect you to be either. And, most importantly, I have to give you the break that you don't have to be like me.

It's hard to digest this because we really, really want to "change others" and help other people to be different (i.e. like *us*!). As I said, when I talk about abandoning the need to change other people, it's interesting how many people resist the idea. "But I need to change them! I can't let them just go along being as difficult as they are. They need me to change them!"

Here we find ourselves right back at Secret Number One, where it's all about *me*. Who says I do have the best ideas? The best approach? The best ideas about changing you? When we really think about it, it's almost laughable, but it's an idea we all hold near and dear.

Step Outside the Theatre

A wise mentor of mine, Dr. Richard Harte, author of "What's Keeping Your Customers Up at Night?", once taught me about the Theatre of Oneself — the idea that we're always on the stage in our lives, acting out our role in relation to someone else acting in their role. So, we believe we are being "real" and authentic, but we are actually putting on a performance in each and every interaction we have with another person. We fall into typical roles and typical behaviors, oftentimes (most times) unconsciously, not realizing that we're playing a role.

Mastering the art of stepping out of the theatre means that right in the middle of a discussion or an interaction, we start to notice ourselves — notice the other person — and notice what we're doing. Instead of getting caught up in responding the way we always respond, or doing what we always do, we step outside and see ourselves acting and reacting. I call this process becoming an "Interested Observer" (IO) and it can be so hard to do, especially when I'm entrenched in my position.

We encounter those "triggers" in our lives and before we know it we have stepped out onto the stage, again, and are acting in the role that we've assumed many times before. The IO position says, "Here I am and I'm about to do what I've done 1,000 times before. Let me view myself doing this and decide whether I want to take that next step — that I've always taken or, instead, take a different step this time."

Again, we learn a lot when we can instill the discipline to be an IO in our most volatile, or difficult situations: the boss who upsets us, the spouse who "always pushes buttons," and the friend who irritates us every time they start down a certain path of discussion. For me, it's my 12-year-old daughter. She has been my best teacher about my own theatre, because she knows how to push my buttons!

Watch What's Happening

If you catch yourself and give yourself the chance to step outside (remember we're talking about doing this stepping out mentally; don't really physically do this while you are talking to someone or they'll think you're avoiding them — it's all about them!), it's interesting to see how robotic we are and how often we have set patterns of interacting. There is tremendous freedom when we realize that we can be an IO, watching what's happening instead of being sucked down into it. We can choose, at any point in time, to drop the role that we are playing and put a focus on the other person. See their needs, their pain, their experience, and realize what we are doing to contribute to the difficulty in our interaction. The act of dropping our need to be right, right in the middle of an exchange, is an exhilarating experience. It takes the pressure off both of us.

Think about any parenting book, marriage book, and general problem-solving book — if we were to tell the truth, we pick them up hoping to get some insight into how to better understand, and communicate with (read: change), our significant other or child or co-worker. We want them to think, talk, act, and *be* like us, or at least we want them to do things in a way that we can understand and manage. Our kids, our spouse, our boss, and our annoying friend frustrate us simply because they won't do what we want them to do. Once I accept the fact that they may never do what I want them to do, things do become much easier to deal with. If I can fundamentally understand that the other people out there are no less "okay" than I am — and are struggling with many of the same issues inside that I am — I have a chance to become a person of compassion.

Someone reading this book may say, "But you don't understand — my mother-in-law really is a terrible person!", or "My boss is impossible!" To that, I would say, they may be. It still doesn't mean that you have to change to negative behavior on your part in order to deal with them. Most "difficult" people are missing something deep inside. They haven't found a better way to fill a void so they fill it with their difficult natures. Once you can step outside and understand this, you are the one released from their difficulties! I once taught a coaching client of mine about the imaginary Plexiglas she could erect around herself when her boss came after her with his anger. And, as I continued to advise her, if the Plexiglas didn't work for her, she had the choice to walk away from that boss and that job.

Confronting Thoughtfully

I'm not advocating that we never confront anyone about anything, but that we confront them thoughtfully and with an understanding of what we really want to accomplish and why it's important to address their behavior. After we've had a chance to process whether it is really a problem that you can't live with (i.e. a husband beating one of the children who doesn't behave), or it's my problem but it harms no one else if someone wants to do something differently (i.e. a child who wants to sleep with their head at the foot of the bed), then we know what our course of action should be.

Think about how many times you've let someone else know they are not okay doing what they are doing because you just don't agree with their behavior. Now, when you stop to think about it, who have they hurt with what they are doing? Is it really worth fighting about with someone, or is it because of a need you have to make that other person be just like you?

Gossip and blame are both detrimental responses that arise from trying to show the world that you're okay, but the other people out there are not. Why do we have an opinion about what someone else does or the choices they make (gossip)? Why do we have a need to point a finger at someone who has done something that disrupts our life (blame)? Because we need to keep the image in place that we're okay and — to do so — others cannot be okay. Somehow we've developed a belief that in order to build ourselves up, we have to tear others down. It's a cycle that, once set in motion, guarantees that no one feels "okay."

Dropping your need to have everyone else be in the wrong, while you are okay, allows you to have the chance to open the door to true communication. Just for the sport of it, next time you are really mad or distressed or frustrated — don't react. Don't yell, don't pout, don't dash off a nasty e-mail, but instead let the feelings sit for 72 hours — yes, for three days. See if you are still feeling as strongly about whatever the issue was at the end of that time. If so, then act on it — and if not, let it go!

If we spent nearly as much time turning the light onto our own thoughts, our own feelings, and our own experience of inadequacy as we do shining it in the eyes of others to highlight their inadequacies, the world would truly be a better place to be (my filter and judgment). One thing is for sure, if we spent the time exploring our own inner feelings and our own reactions to others and to our daily experiences, we'd have no time to worry about what other people are thinking or doing.

Maybe Others Don't Need to be "Fixed"

In general, for most of us, it is hard for us to let other people be "okay" as they are and to accept them. We tend to want to fix everybody — in their own best interest, of course. Although our filters block our view, we think we see so clearly what someone else needs to do differently.

And there may be times we are pained from watching people we care about being hurt or in trouble. There may be the friend who is being abused by the overbearing boss, the sister who is about to marry the "wrong guy," the child who is feeling depressed because someone is picking on them.

There are many people who need our compassion and our understanding that we encounter each day. Needing compassion and understanding is very different from being told you are doing something wrong, or that you need to change to be a better person.

If you've ever had the experience where you did see someone you care about doing something "wrong" and wanted to help that person, you will know that if the person isn't open to help — they won't hear a word you are saying. They will just feel "admonished" by you. So we have to ask ourselves, why we do feel the need to let others know our disapproval with what they choose to do in the life that belongs to them? Oftentimes it is because we want to feel better about ourselves — it's that deep down "I'm not okay" problem rearing up again. If I don't feel completely okay with me, but I point out how really NOT okay you are, then (by default), I must be better than you!

And, again, I am not advocating that we don't address things with people, or express our experience of something in the relationship. We just need to be sure we are doing so for the right reasons. Not because of clouded filters, or the need to be right, but rather because we are able to reach a higher level of relationship together. Many times if someone else's behavior is a problem to us, it's because we haven't asked ourselves, "What about this behavior pushes my buttons?" If we can look at the behavior more objectively — become the IO stepping out of the theatre, we'll learn a lot about ourselves as well as others around us.

Imagine how relationships would change if we could practice leaving other people alone — practice refraining from pointing out their weaknesses — and instead practice what we need to do to clear our own filters, understand our own cloudy viewpoint and generally do our own internal work.

It's hard work most assuredly, but the payoff is worth it when we find ourselves freed from the need to correct everyone else in the futile effort to find peace and feel "okay."

Being Okay — It's Hard Work!

The truth is that it's all hard work — becoming more confident and "okay" with who I am, becoming more aware of who you are, and giving up the need to change the person on the other side of the relationship. Dropping all of it sounds easy, but in fact it's some of the hardest work we'll ever do. It's so much easier to move along in our blissful state, thinking that we're right and wanting to spend our time changing others. Dropping the need to do this all day every day is very freeing, but we may feel a void because we've so traditionally filled it with our negative experiences of other people.

If we all took a bit of time each day to step outside of our own theatre, and to become an Interested Observer, we'd often see how silly our beliefs and our behaviors really are with one another. One of the most productive things I've ever learned is, in the middle of a difficult discussion with someone where we're both entrenched in our position, to start to laugh about it. Not to laugh about the other person, of course, but to laugh about how we've become attached to our viewpoints and unwilling to move. If I drop my need to be "okay" while making you "not okay" and see the whole exchange as funny, it takes away anyone's need to be right. We start working together to find a common solution, or a common decision.

None of us are really "okay" — we're all doing the best that we can with limited resources and very limited understanding of how best to be in relationship with one another. If we can accept the Five Secrets, and accept that we all have work we need to do in order to be more authentic, compassionate people, then we can begin to have real change happen in our lives and truly be "okay."

What to Do? Step Outside Your Theatre

Realizing that everyone — including you — is doing the best with what they have to work with today, try these steps for dealing with Secret Number Five:

1. Step outside your own theatre several times a day. Put on the hat of detective or IO (Interested Observer). When you are in an interaction with someone, drop your need to be right (both in your own mind and in what you're expressing to them) about what's happening, and instead watch how you are behaving and what's really going on in the exchange. Be more interested in what's transpiring between the two of you, than you are in your position and your need to state your case and get your point across. Generally start seeing what's happening in your life objectively

and with a desire to learn. Become watchful of who you are and what you do and watch others, too.

2. Recognize that you're okay; you're just where you need to be and how you need to be at this point in time. We're all working on things, and while we may "know" what to do, very few of us actually manage to do it every hour of every day. So each time you let yourself down, get back up and give yourself a break—and then start again to become a more authentic person.

3. Give others a break, too. None of us are perfect, and the truth is that most people are trying their best. We haven't learned communicating well, or feeling good about ourselves, or giving others the benefit of our positive assumptions. Imagine how your life would change if you just repeated that mantra every day—"I know you *are* trying your best." Say it silently to everyone you interact with, and you'll find you approach them differently.

Secret Number One:
It's All About ME!

Secret Number Two:
Our Behavioral Styles Come Between Us

Secret Number Three:
Your Values Speak Louder Than You Do

Secret Number Four:
Don't Assume I Know What You Mean

Secret Number Five:
I'm Okay, You Are Most Definitely NOT Okay

**Putting It All Together:
What To Do Next**

Putting It All Together:
What to Do Next?

So you've spent the time to read this book, and perhaps you've stopped at every section and practiced implementing the steps to change for each of the Five Secrets. What's next?

This can be just another book you've read, and maybe you've learned something, maybe you haven't. You can walk away knowing what you need to do and choosing not to do it, or you can walk away and commit that you will at least experiment with some of these ideas. Change is hard. We like to stay with what we already know and convince ourselves it's "right" for us (because after all, it *is* all about *me!*). Don't do that to yourself or to others. Make it your work to become a detective in your own life. See where you are jumping to conclusions, labeling others, and moving so quickly that you don't focus on what someone else is really all about — and what they are trying to communicate to you. Take the time to step back — work at understanding yourself first and seeing where you can make changes to become more effective, before you spend time trying to change other people.

Recognize that we do have our filters. We do have our own behavioral style and approach, and we do have unique values that drive us. When we communicate, we are each expressing our own style with our values deeply rooted in what we believe is right. If your style differs from mine, and your values are at odds with what I care about, communication and understanding are going to take us both a lot of effort and giving.

And even once we get past the style and values differences, remember that I still can't understand everything you mean because I'm not you. When you give me small pieces of information, snippets of what you want me to understand, but you don't provide me the context and background for why it matters — you don't give me the chance to really understand you.

While you are talking to me, know that even though I may be approaching you with bravado and a forthright statement in our exchange, the truth is I don't believe — deep down — that I'm okay, or that you are either.

IAAM: It's All About Me!

Remember Secret Number One — "It's All About Me," when you are thinking about what others are saying or doing instead of listening to them, or viewing what's happening with a "that's right, that's wrong" attitude. Catch yourself when you're lost in your own thoughts or planning what you'll say next or secretly disagreeing with what's being communicated to you. Recognize you are doing these things, and then make a decision to just drop it. Just leave the need to assess everything, judge everything, and label everything — it's an exhausting process we put ourselves through every day! Remember this secret when you want to rail at someone else about their "self-involvement" — after all, it *is* all about me to most of us.

Don't use this with your spouse or child to say, "*See*, it's all about you!" Of course it is — it is for all of us. All we can do is take responsibility for our role in it and make different choices. We can only focus on what we need to do differently and, as difficult as it is to accept, we really can't change other people and make them act the way we want them to. As a hypnotist, I know that we can plant seeds in the subconscious mind and work with a client to help them embrace new ways of thinking, but ultimately — even with the best scripting we have in our toolbox — the person has to want to change. If someone who seeks help from me has a difficult time with change, how is it going to go with the person who didn't want to change in the first place? It *is* all about me for me, and it's all about you for you. Once we own that this is true, we can start to make different choices about how we'll approach others.

I Like You — If You're Like Me!

Remember that Secret Number Two — "Our behavioral styles come between us" — can be applied when you see or feel a difference in communication style and approach. When you have the experience that the "click" just isn't there and somehow you aren't getting through, pay attention to tone of voice, to the pace people use and the words they use. Watch the style of others — listen carefully, and watch their emotional response to things, or lack thereof. You don't want to label ("Oh, *he* is a high D!"), but rather to work to understand what the other person is communicating to you about themselves so that you can observe the differences and, where you choose, adapt and modify to meet their style.

Remember that you aren't trying to be someone you are not, but you are trying to make efforts to understand and be understood by those you care about. Recognize that other styles can work equally as well as your own, and that sometimes you may benefit from someone's style and approach even when it differs from yours. We get stuck in our style, and seeing another way sometimes gives us options we may not have otherwise had.

Your Hidden Values are Very Loud!

The Values discussed in Secret Number Three will become clear when you are disagreeing with someone or having a hard time understanding why they do things the way they do, or make decisions the way they do. Our values underlie our decisions and our approach to life, and they are firmly entrenched for most of us. Don't try to figure out for others what they should do, or how they should behave. Don't judge them because their decisions and approach differ from yours — continue to make the choice to drop your need to be right. It doesn't mean giving up what you care about. Of course, your values are right — for you. Leave it at that and choose to leave others' values alone.

Help Me with Some Context

"Don't assume I know what you mean," Secret Number Four, is so important in relationships, working situations, interviews, etc. Stop putting information out there and expecting the other person to just pick it up and know what you mean! Be more like a teacher and provide context — why, where, how, and what led you to a certain conclusion. Explain why it matters and, if you can't figure out a reason why it matters, consider that it doesn't matter to anyone else but you. Be more conscious of how you communicate and what you communicate to others, and take the time to check for understanding.

Refresh yourself on active listening and reflective statements to be sure that communication is passing both ways. Also put time in to work on being a clear and strong communicator. Be sure you've been heard and understood, and resolve to be very careful when making assumptions about anyone or anything.

I Really AM Okay?

Finally, Secret Number Five is one to keep close in your consciousness at all times. Remember that even though I may show something else to the world, deep down I believe that I'm really not okay. As such, everything you do to reinforce this, to be unkind to me, and to show me how wrong I am, simply reminds me of what I already fear — that something inside of me is missing and I'm not really as good as I want to be. We need to work to bring the best aspect of other people out, instead of crushing their spirits down all of the time. Build a sense of "okay" inside of yourself before you go out and try to build it in others. The more you practice any of these secrets and some of the communication techniques, the more you will find yourself really, truly feeling okay with yourself and with others.

Begin to Do Your Own Work

As they say in Alcoholics Anonymous — the first step is to acknowledge the problem. So if you decide to take the time to acknowledge the truth of what you've read here, and once you've taken something in and understood it to be true for you, begin to make small changes every day. Remember, any new behavioral change needs 21 days of consistency to be reinforced and to become part of a natural approach. Even if on one or two occasions each day you don't react from the "filter-driven" place, but rather from a place of observation and thoughtfulness, you'll allow yourself an entirely new experience. You may even find that you like it.

Take some time out of each day to become aware of how you are interacting with someone else — watch for your filters, observe behavioral style, listen to the values disconnect, work to help them understand, and don't "assume," and realize that they're really not feeling okay — and neither are you! Realize that sometimes you're putting your burdens onto someone else, hoping they will take them away from you — when really all you are doing is adding to the burdens they already have.

If you pay attention to the Five Secrets and practice even just a little bit with one each day, you'll see changes in the responses and reactions you get from others. Things won't change overnight, but if you are working with a system, and using the set of tools you have just learned, you're increasing your chances of working with, communicating with, and living with other people more effectively.

And when you've tried any one of the Five Secrets and made progress — please write to me and let me know!

Acknowledgements

It's impossible to thank all of the people throughout my life who have provided the support, insight, and ideas that have become the basis for this book. Most especially I want to thank all of you with whom I practiced very poor communication and showed a lack of understanding about what you were trying to say. Please know that by making those mistakes, I learned a lot about what I should, and shouldn't, do.

About the Author

Beverly D. Flaxington holds both a BSBA and an MBA from Suffolk University and is now an adjunct professor at Suffolk in the undergraduate and graduate programs, teaching Small Business Management, Organizational Behavior, Leadership and Social Responsibility and Dealing With Difficult People. She has run her own business consulting firm, The Collaborative, since 1995.

In 2008, she and her consulting partner cofounded AdvisorsTrustedAdvisor.com, a site dedicated to the needs of financial advisors. Bev is a Certified Professional Behavioral Analyst and Certified Professional Values Analyst, and works with the DISC and PIAV tools. She has been a Certified Hypnotist and Certified Hypnosis Trainer for over 15 years. She works both in corporate settings and one-on-one with individuals to help them manage their stress and meet individual, career, and corporate goals. She is also an accomplished trainer and public speaker. Beverly is the author of *The 7 Steps to Effective Business Building for Financial Advisors,* coauthor of *Wealthbuilding: A Consumer's Guide to Making Profitable — and Comfortable — Investment Decisions,* published by Dearborn Financial Publishing.

Wealthbuilding was a Book of the Month Club Money Club selection.

Bev lives in Massachusetts with her three children, four dogs, and four cats.

For More Information

To deepen your communication and people skills, please visit **www.UnderstandingOtherPeople.com** or call **1-888-580-9473 (WISE)**.

Bev is a highly sought after national speaker, to invite her to speak to your group please call **1-888-580-9473 (WISE)**, or by using the information below:

Beverly Flaxington, Principal
The Collaborative
P.O. Box 71
Medfield MA, 02052

www.the-collaborative.com
info@the-collaborative.com